New Eyes with Which to See

"Give me new eyes with which to see the New Year, Lord. Give me new and clearer vision. Let me bring new awareness to all the dear and precious sights and sounds . . .

"You have made the world so incredibly lovely. You have lavished your artistry not only on the mountains in their majesty, the seas in their splendor, the forests in their grandeur—but on the simplest, humblest things about me: A mud puddle in the sun. A child with a pair of skates. The peeling door of an abandoned house. A single tree.

"Thank you for all these wonders, Lord. For those I have witnessed in the past, and all those that await me in this exciting New Year."

—MARJORIE HOLMES
from *BEAUTY IN YOUR OWN BACKYARD*

Bantam Books by Marjorie Holmes
Ask your bookseller for the books you have missed

Marjorie Holmes

Beauty in Your Own Backyard

BANTAM BOOKS · TORONTO · NEW YORK · LONDON

BEAUTY IN YOUR OWN BACKYARD
*A Bantam Book / published by arrangement with
EPM Publications, Inc.*

PRINTING HISTORY
*EPM edition published October 1976
Better Homes and Gardens Book Club Alternate October 1976
A Selection of the Christian Herald Book Club
Bantam edition / March 1980*

ACKNOWLEDGMENT
The author wishes to thank the
Washington *Star* for permission
to include material from her
Love and Laughter column.

ISBN 0-553-11429-8

Published simultaneously in the United States and Canada

This book is lovingly dedicated to the memory of my first English teacher *Dewey Deal* who urged: "If you want to badly enough you can write beautiful things for people who crave beautiful things. *There is a duty.*"

Contents

Spring

Before the Curtain Rises

This is the time between seasons. It is the time of waiting, as between the acts of a play.

The earth's costume is drab. It looks stripped down to its underwear. Yet there is a subtle richness here. A sense of thrilled waiting. Of suspenseful pause before the drama to come.

The brittle bones of the trees sway restlessly, as if the sap were wine-like in the veins. Scatter rugs of snow hang in the hills. The ground is spongy to the feet, and the green is straining through the old brown-yellowed-gray of its grasses. There is mud, and the shape of half-rotted leaves pressed into it. The hedges are a dry nothingness of hue, faded, stubbly and sere.

The sky is swathed in clouds the color of skimmed milk, bluish and thin—but here and there is a gash where the deeper blue shows through.

This is the colorless time, when even the houses have not yet had their bright new flauntings of paint; when even the smoke they emit is a half-hearted thing, not vibrant and rolling and hot-dark as so recently.

Yet there is a gentle suspense in the air. A softness as of coming rain. A suggestion of the secret sap that traces its course in the trees. Of buds about to break and birds about to return. Of ripeness and warmth to spill forth the more fully for this very waiting. Of swiftly unfolding scenes whose delight will be heightened by this very period of withholding—this quiet, colorless, promising time before the curtain goes up on spring!

When the Seasons Call

The weatherman has predicted a dreary weekend. But today is so bright, so sun-gilded you refuse to believe it. And so when your husband calls to say, "I can't get a thing done at the office, think I'll take my work to the cabin—wanta go?" you wrestle only briefly with all you should be doing, and pack up pets and children.

Simply walking out on duties and difficulties seems to solve them. And the farther the distance between you, the more your sense of guilt diminishes. You feel as free as the sailing clouds, as light as the tossing branches just beginning to be dusted with a hint of budding green along the way.

The cabin smells like a spicebox as you unlock. The logs are the color of honey, mellow and old. You go around flinging windows wide and getting reacquainted with possessions—battered pewter on the mantel, a bean pot still holding last fall's brittle flowers. Bright cushions, half-read books, a jug of paintbrushes, the rag rugs and rustic chairs that echo—something.

What is it? you wonder, smelling the pine, the logs, the fire beginning to crackle in the old stone fireplace. The pioneer in people, perhaps. The need to return to the earth, touch soil, breathe distance and forage for the physical.

And putting the groceries away, bustling about domestic duties that here take on something fresh and challenging from the very limitations, you notice your husband's brisk step as he hauls water, carries firewood, goes through the primitive acts of getting his family warm and secure against the drawing darkness of the woods.

"Well," he says, "it's too late to get at that office work tonight, I'll tackle it tomorrow. Want me to catch us some fish for supper?"

He is whistling as he gathers up the tackle, starts toward the float. The late March wind seems to join him, swaggering around the corner like a bold and jaunty boy. Birds twitter and cheer as they scoop across the water, and the little tree frogs known as peepers, tune up, trying their best to make you think it's time for crickets and katydids and the entire chorus of spring.

And you sense, in some deep area of your being, that this must be really why you came. We are like the creatures; our instincts stir us into action when the seasons change. We too feel this irresistible impulse to emerge from hibernation, fly, forage, scurry, clean, restore our nests or build new ones, take care of our young.

Lingering Legacy

At the lake, at the end of a bright spring day, you stand watching the sun descend.

It has lost its early morning spirit of blazing abandon. It is subdued now, a flower of silver-gold that recedes in a soft melting between the black branches of the trees. Back and back it glides, making its graceful exit, drawing its own reflection along below it on the water.

The lake is a blue-gray mirror, satiny, opaque. It does not want to lose this lovely adornment. It seems to hold it, to cling to the receding sun with liquid hands. But now the sun is nearly gone, above and below; it is a shining echo behind the trees. Leaving only a pale patina of itself, it has vanished into the gray rocks.

Yet the water still holds the frail, lovely image of the trees. Above it they stand in silhouette against the sky, a thousand black pen-strokes, a lacey tracing, remote and far—though the water offers up their image close and clear. It has taken the highest pointy peaks of them and reversed them so that they splay in loveliness at your feet.

What a pity there is no real sunset, you think. No color. Only this muted blending of silver-gold, blue and gray. Then, you see that the sun has left a legacy of pure crimson in the east. As if too modest to wear its own bright banners, it has flung them behind before slipping away.

Look Up at the Trees

Often we live for years without ever noticing how tall, how incredibly tall are some of our nearest trees. Those in your own backyard may go soaring to monumental heights unobserved. Taller than a church steeple, tall as a many-stories building. Yet strongly balanced, reaching down into the earth where their roots hold fast against storm and wind.

Look up and watch them as they sway. Lie down on your back on the floor or a sofa some day and watch them on a windy day. How rhythmic they are, tossed this way and that in a kind of calm, controlled abandon.

How beautiful are the upper reaches of bare branches, their lovely black fretwork sketched against a gull-colored sky. And with what abandoned grace and serenity they sway. "Do with us what you will," they seem to be telling the wind. "We are instruments to your fingers. Pluck us, strum us, create with us whatever music you have in mind."

Or they are naked dancers moving across the stage of the sky. They glide and turn to the movements of the wind's vast symphony.

Soon they will be clothed, the leaves will cover them. The buds are already prickling and stirring.

Then they will seem less free, less tall, however beautiful their draperies. So to comprehend their true height and graceful strength, look up, admire them. Especially on a windy, rainy March day.

The Love Season

Spring is the love season. The time of the sweet restless stirrings. The whole world seems to tremble with some subtle yet strong emotion, unspoken yet singing, expressed in lovely pantomimes more eloquent than words from a stage.

The birds dip about, twittering and flirting, carrying on their courtships on rails and wires and in the frail new leaves. Like an anxious suitor the woodpecker raps his sharp staccato, pauses, tips his head and peers inside. Will it suit her, this hole he is drilling? Or is she already there, his little mate? The swallows swoop eagerly back and forth under the eaves. There is something both merry and worried about their nest building; an open secret they beg us to respect.

The bluebirds are house-hunting. We've built two new homes to attract them, and one day, to our delight, there is a flash of blue and rose on a nearby branch. One perches there while the other descends to inspect. He circles, lands on the roof, hovers over the hole, then flies off to consult his mate. We hold our breaths. Will he return, at least look inside? Horray! He's back, and this time ventures in. Presently he pops out, and it's his partner's turn. We watch like anxious landlords—will they take it? And when they fly off, we feel rejected.

In a few days, however, they are back, like a honeymoon pair who have gone home to pick up a few things before moving in. We rejoice. "Bluebirds mean happiness," we tell each other.

Spring is the love season. The time when the sap is rising in the trees and the blood tingles sweet in the veins. When the very rains in the night seem to whisper of love and union and caressing, of new life to come. A friend from Tiberius writes of the Galilee rains: "The earth here is just waiting for the softening rains to open it out like Japanese paper flowers in a saucer of water."

Even the flowers when they burst into bloom are bridal, dressed in their finest, yielding to the assault of the bees. Listen to the fierce love humming as the bees drink their nectar and take the pollen for the mating.

And people too—we quicken to the call of spring. Spring speaks to us, stirs us, woos us. It is not only "a young man's fancy" that "turns to thoughts of love." We turn instinctively to love whatever our age, to memories of past loves (we can't forget them—why should we?—they are part of our life stories) ; and to thoughts of our beloved today.

House Fixing Is a Self-Portrait

However she may protest its often frustrating aspects, happy is the woman who has a house to fix.

For a house, even more than her children, is the expression of herself. A child has his own nature to assert. He looks the way the good Lord made him. And more often than not he *won't* be made into the image you have of him, no matter how hard you try.

Houses too can be contrary, yes. It takes money to fashion them into the ultimate backgrounds we visualize. For some people quite a lot of money; for others with imagination, determination and energy, far less.

But no matter how much or how little money is spent, the secret of making a home that reflects the individual personality is simply *caring* enough to take the time. Time to comb the shops for materials to make the curtains and cushions and spreads. Going to the bother of prowling through stores, whether new or second-hand, to track down a cupboard or cabinet you can "just see" in a certain spot. Piling the small fry into the car and spending a day at a country auction. Sewing or painting or fixing or fussing long after they're in bed.

This does not necessarily mean that you need to do so, for economy's sake. No, the need is even more compelling; a need that is shared just as intensely by people of means: the desire to create something truly lovely out of your surroundings. To write or paint or draw a kind of daily song or picture of yourself!

Sunday Drive

How lovely is a Sunday in the spring!

The trees hurl high their shining arms. All are ribbed and rimmed with silver, every arch and branch and twig. Bright from its winter bondage, the very sun seems to sing.

There is a spirit of release, a sense of freedom in the fields as you fly past them in the car. Gray and sodden in tones of gunmetal or sluggish tan, relieved only by sudden, tawny bronze stretches, yet you feel the wind go prancing across them, trying to rouse them, abandoned and gay.

The very clouds that sweep across the sky are triumphant, upswinging, like long-limbed dancers flinging high their filmy scarves.

The sun pours along the pavement, festooned by the looping shadows of the wires along its banks.

A stream goes nosing through the hills, wearing a glassy scalloped petticoat of ice. White ducks sink into its black shining waters, or walk gingerly, like fearful old men, upon its slippery rim.

Nature's Feisty Family

Sometimes even nature seems like a family, with all its personalities contesting for attention.

The day starts out cloudy, mist-hung. Birds sing but warily. A few drops patter on the trees. Then toward noon the sun bursts through. Everything sparkles and shines. But just when the sun seems firmly in command, clouds appear like some powerful authority that say, "Now, now, this can't go on!" Or, "What's this? We had things all worked out—what's happening?"

Thunder reinforces them; they speak in growling voices, crack whips. Lightning flashes, even as the obstinate sun holds firm. The rain comes blasting down, yet the sun persists. Patiently smiling, it claims its portion of the sky. And even when driven off altogether, the sun slips back with some banners of scarlet as if to set its flag of victory upon the day.

But the rain responds with fervor renewed. It pounds its fists, pours down, rushing the world, wrapping it up in sheets. Sky and water and woods and trees belong to it the evening long. At last, feeling perhaps it has won, it tapers off. There is only a misty dripping, a sense of some cozy compromise.

Yet now the moon has risen. A full moon, warmly golden, ready to reign. Through the veils it pours its lovely light. On water still restless and rain-riddled, its perfection lies. You look out and there it is, the round yellow pearl of the moon trembling on the water at your feet.

And all night long this contest continues—the moon smiling blandly and stubbornly down in its glory while the rain strives. You waken toward morning to find the moon moved far over but weaker now, and the rain intensified. By morning the rain has won, so it seems. The world is gray, the rain resting but standing in readiness. You wonder how soon the sun will rise to the challenge, and the beautiful battle will be resumed.

Cardinals at Sunset

The sun is beginning its descent: its slanting rays pour across the water and gild the tossing heads of trees.

You are sitting on the balcony with a book and this bright falling loveliness is all about you, warm and peaceful yet lively—softly lively as you firmly hold down the pages that respond to the breeze. They are almost alive to the radiance, they too want to lift and bend and stir to the slanting breeze-tossed light.

And to the left, just below, where the rocks pitch down to the water and there are many saplings and greeny growths, you are aware of a sudden new brightness. A bloody brightness poised on a leafy branch almost near enough to touch. A male cardinal, light-enhanced. From the cocky crest to the tip of his tilting tail he is a scarlet flame. And a little beyond him, hesitant, like a wife in patient pursuit, is perched his mate.

And her smaller drab brown body is radiant too, pink in the light, with her touches of red at beak and breast aflame. And their rosiness, the torchy glow of both these two, is echoed in the delicate pendants of the maple tree above them. It is a small tree, not very old, thin-branched, ruddy and new with promise, its delicate preview of leaves.

The leaves are formed, they hang on it like little dancing umbrellas, with this fluttery glory of coral pendants dangling to make a gay canopy for the birds.

It is one of those moments of unexpected beauty, so perfect in every detail that you wish you could catch it, keep it, frame it to show to others or look back upon again. Yet it is the very evanescence of the picture that enhances its charm. In a few moments the cardinal zooms away, streaking off into the sunset, his mate following. And the sun has vanished behind the trees.

The Old Familiar Teakettle

It sits a little cockeyed on the stove—your old familiar whistling teakettle.

Its sides are nicked and scratched and it wears its lid at a rakish angle, and when it summons you these days its voice is a cross between a shriek and a sigh.

You lift it up to fix the coffee and your mind goes back, for no good reason, to the origin of this faithful little servant you reach for so blindly a dozen times a day.

And you remember a certain birthday, and an eagerly hovering bright-eyed boy. And his proud announcement as the gift wrappings fell away and its shining glory was revealed: "I won it playing bingo. That night Daddy took me to the 'musement park. And we had this secret—we'd hide it till your birthday, under the bed."

You remember his rapturous sigh, and how eagerly he dashed to the kitchen with it and filled it with cold water and tried to cope with the stove. And his anxiety over the interminable time it took before the kettle began to purr softly, as if tuning up, then to whistle its chipper triumphant tune.

Dear little kettle, you think. How gay you were in the beginning. How bright your sides, how sweet your song. And we've taken you so for granted, we've scarcely noticed the change in you.

You set it down on the sink and try to regard it with dispassionate eyes; its tarnish, its scars of living. Really you ought to replace it, you inform yourself. Teakettles are on sale right now.

But instead you find yourself taking up a scouring pad to scrub it. You scrub it with loving vigor, this old whistling teakettle. . . . A little bit the way you used to scrub the grubby face of a young whistling boy.

Pussy Willows

One of the nicest things to have in a yard is a pussy willow tree.

The slender fronds of the willows arch like the arms of young mothers gathered to cuddle their babies against the cold. Then one fine day your little boy cries, "Look, look, the pussy willows are coming out!" And sure enough, each tight little red-brown cradle is beginning to open; at each pointed tip peeps a tiny pearl-gray head.

He breaks off a few of the moist, rosy-green wands, and brings them inside. You give him a jar to place on a sunny window sill. Within the hour, the furry-soft little creatures have crept shyly forth, almost purring.

The next day more are picked for school. You watch him trot proudly off with his nodding treasures, and friends gathering about to admire. You can barely see the cowlicky head above the school bus window, but the branches bob a gay goodbye . . .

You can almost smell the schoolroom with its pencil shavings, crayons, varnished desks, and see the blue jug the teacher put them in. Almost hear the thick green construction paper being passed out, the whisper of pinky chalk and russet brown as small artists labor lovingly over the still life that will be today's art lesson . . .

Your own tall pitcher of pussy willows lasts for weeks. Like the real cats that drowse in the sun, they wax and grow fat. Then they turn golden—a frail dusting that sheds like fairy stuff.

Spring Planting

You sit on the porch after dinner with a cup of coffee, letting the spring evening fall softly around your shoulders like a stole.

Nearby your husband is setting our azaleas. Kneeling, he scoops earth, lifts the plum salmon pink bushes, and pats and firms and comforts them into their new homes. So small now, little and shy as children, you visualize the vivid spreading of their arms in years to come.

The hydrangeas are blooming along the fence. Fluffy confections—like popcorn balls dyed carnival colors, ink-blue, lavender, pink. The primroses are yellow flames at their feet. And white and lacey along hill and lane and roadway the doilies of the dogwoods are strewn.

Still sipping at the warm companionable coffee, you take a little tour checking on seeds planted last week. Anxious, always apprehensive. (If, like me you're better at admiring other people's flowers than raising your own.) Hooray, the zinnias are up! Good old zinnias, like dependable but rather pushy people who've always got to be first. The marigolds are more reticent—barely pricking through, although your husband's potted variety are already a banner of gold. And the pansies are a velvety abundance.

You pick the pansies, and finishing your coffee,

use the mug for a holder. They crowd it jauntily, their monkey faces peering over its earthen rim. Geraniums blaze beside the walk, giving off a bitter-sweet fragrance in the fast-falling dusk—and dressed to match the cardinal, who calls good-night as it flashes home.

People Who Like Flowers

You and your husband stop at a roadside nursery to pick up "a few plants." Some peppers and tomatoes, and maybe a few more Impatiens plants. But climbing out you are assailed by a madness, a riot of color, a carpeting of pink and purple and white and brilliant, indescribable hues. They burst from their baskets, they stream in all directions like stripes in a banner.

"Oh, my goodness, I had no idea you had all this!" you exclaim to the proprietor, who smiles back at you, all rosy and bursting with the joy of it, like the flowers.

He wears stained khaki pants and a faded shirt of blue, his cheeks are pink as the azaleas, his eyes the color of cornflowers.

"Yes, we've got just about everything you'd want," he beams, gesturing to this fairyland that flanks the busy, burning highway.

"Impatiens plants? They're sometimes hard to find."

"There you are—pick 'em out. Now this is nice, such a deep salmon pink. Looks good enough to eat."

"How about daisies?" you suddenly remember.

"Follow me."

On your way you pause to hover over the petunias—enormous fluted blossoms, like girls in ruffled sunbonnets. And the pansies. "What in the world do you feed them to make them so big?" You pass another customer trundling a bright green wheelbarrow laden with beauties unknown. "Excuse me, but what are those? They look like artificial roses."

"Yes, don't they?" the woman exclaims. "They're balsam. They grow waist-high and bloom like crazy all summer long."

"Oh, we must have some." You consult the man about their habits and needs.

"And these geraniums," your husband says, squatting beside the lush bursts of scarlet and flame. "Let's get some for a window box. Summer just wasn't summer without geraniums in a window box back home."

And the proprietor echoes yes, yes, it was that way in his boyhood, too. And he sorts and serves up the brightest, the fattest, the choicest of everything that strikes your fancy. And throws in a few extra for good measure.

"I always want to make sure people get what they pay for and a little bit more," he says. "There's just something about dealing with people who like flowers. . . ."

People who like flowers. . . . The battered hat pushed to the back of the perspiring forehead, rosy with sun and pleasure. . . . The thick brown hands so gently helping you carry them to the car. . . . You will think of him again when you look out your window viewing the brilliance he has helped bring into your yard.

Spring's Palette

At your feet the violets grow. Like frail tinted stars they sprinkle the whole yard, from pale lavender to deep purple; they splay down the hummocky toes of a giant tree.

In earnest concentration the children squat to pick them, like living bouquets themselves with their gay jerseys and yellow hair. The shadows of the trees lace the lawn and the white board fence. Scarlet petunias are a bright shout of color beside the old stone house.

All about you the hills flow away, pale green and taupe, with copses of deeper green woods and pointed fir trees. While everywhere is the white foam of apple and cherry blossoms.

Cattle come up to the fence and stand blandly watching the children crouching among the violets. A breeze causes a little storm of petals from the trees. You go inside at last with your arms full of blooms, white and delicate pink, and their fragrance fills the house. Later, jelly glasses and little pots of children's posies are displayed like jewels on the windowsills.

The Dogwoods and the Cross

Earlier and earlier each evening the dog begins whimpering for her walk. You put her off as long as you can but her plaintive eyes, your own conscience, and sheer habit make you reach for her leash.

"Okay, you win. Come on."

Off she rushes, yanking you after, down the drive and up the curving hill, with pauses every few minutes to squat, snoop, sniff, or joyously paw the leaves that lie beside the road. They rattle, make a merry explosion as she explores them, while you stand, too tired to be impatient, soothed by the cool sweet night.

The round moon floods the sky with a blue-white light. A few stars sparkle, like rare diamonds carefully placed. Beneath them, softly pulsing and winking, glide the colored stars of planes. The trees stand tall, reaching up as if to catch and hold them with their yearning arms. A star is caught here and there in a branch. One of the gliding stars thrusts through and moves on, singing to itself.

The leaves are still frail, little and new, a tremulous dusting upon these tall old trees. And just below them the dogwoods are a mystical new white mist of bloom. They have come suddenly, these blossoms. Only a few days ago a red suggestion of buds, now the flattish, faintly cupped petals are upheld, like some precious display of china in a jeweler's window.

The older dogwoods are rich and heavy with their white treasure. The younger, newer ones stand modest, offering up what they have in a kind of tentative wonder, surprised at their own loveliness.

The moon enhances their translucent purity. The very roadway, dark by day, is white with its flooding, and the white dog, now bounding along ahead, has a luminous quality.

A utility pole beside the road is illuminated too, its black spear and crossbar moon-rimmed. Turning, you see its shadow lying across the moon-white road.

A *cross!* A leaning cross, moon-etched. Tender, graceful, and not really sad. Only touching. A gentle reminder of suffering—all human suffering and triumph on a moonlit roadway on a sweet spring night just before Good Friday.

A Dancey Day

"Oh, this is a dancey day," the middle one says, racing down the steps to the dock and standing, arms wide to the wind. And it truly is. For the wind that has rocked and sung to the cabin all night, like mother to child, has become by morning a mad and merry maid.

It scoops the glittering surface of the water and flings it this way and that, like handfuls of stars. The bright glitter runs before it and seems to leap, as if trying to play with the new leafy tips of the trees. The dogwoods swing and sway like sweet girl graduates in dresses of glossy white. The forsythias fling themselves about and shed their final gold upon the grass.

The children rush this way and that, prancing, cavorting, trying to catch the butterflies that dip above the tossing flowers. You feel your own hair struggling to escape its scarf as you kneel to set out petunias and pansies and fat new baskets of creeping phlox. You break off chunks and strands of the delicate starlike blossoms, and they, too, scamper off, wind-lured. You retrieve them, like naughty runaway children, and press them firmly into their damp little nests in the earth.

And the small fry come scampering up to help. Hair blowing, shirttails flapping, they squat to dig and poke and slop and plant. The sunlight flicks and flashes over their small bright figures. Birds chortle and protest in the merrily dancing trees. The dog bounds after a fancied threat in the swaying rushes. The cat scurries, a streak of silver, up a tree. Two wild ducks go winging across the water, leaning lightly against the breeze.

All the world is prancing and sparkling, tuned to the windy music of the morning. It is indeed a "dancey day!"

A Footbridge for Angels

It begins to rain softly as you finish the dishes. "Good," you say, thinking of the plants you've just set out. "I only wish I'd gotten more into the ground."

The shower quickens, dances brightly, then stops. A pale yellow glow suffuses the sky. Drops wink silver on the green abundance of new leaves. Birds cry out their liquid notes, lovely and clear. The lake below is a luminous sheet of palest gold, traced with glittering triangles where the breeze runs by.

"Oh, boy, I'll bet there'll be a rainbow!" a child says, hurling down a dishtowel and running to the balcony. In a minute the glad announcement comes, "There sure is—come look!"

You join him, and find it arching softly upward from a pink cloud which is rimmed with fire. But only a portion of a rainbow, like a little footbridge for angels—you can see them wisping up its delicate slopes, playing softly around it, then disappearing into the deepening violet colors of the cloud.

"Oh, heck, it's fading," the child objects. "It's practically gone." He's right. The footbridge too is vanishing, being drawn by unseen hands into the mystery from which it came. "Why can't a rainbow LAST?" he demands.

"I suppose if it did we'd get used to it," you tell

him. "We wouldn't notice it anymore, we'd take it for granted."

He leans against the rail a moment, wistfully pondering.

"I get it—half the prettiness of a rainbow is the excitement; no matter how many times you see one it's always a surprise."

Snowing Blossoms

You hear the thunder muttering somewhere behind the swaying trees; the skies begin to glower. "Good, oh good, it's going to rain," you announce. "We need it."

"But look, Mommy, it's started already," a child exclaims. "But it's not raining, it's snowing!"

"Snowing?" Darting to the window, you see that white flakes are indeed coasting down. "No, honey, that's not snow, those are cherry petals," you tell her. "And that reminds me, if we want any for the mantel we'd better hurry. Come on."

Tossing a sweater about your shoulders, you hurry outside, tailed by other crying, "Me, too, I promised some for my teacher," . . . "Can I cut some tulips?" . . . "What about the forsythia? Look, it's shedding, the ground's all covered with gold."

There is a mass foray on the yard. The trees are growing truly anxious before the coming storm—they reach out their lovely laden hands, and you break off branches of bloom. A little boy squats before the tossing cups of the tulips, scarlet and white, or wine-dark as the clouds.

There is a happy sense of hurry, of racing the first bright spats of cool spring rain. Rescue them while you can, these delicate frail young things in their fluffy party frocks, bring them inside where they'll be safe from the lusty ravages to come.

The wind tries to snatch them away. It winds your skirt about your legs and yanks at your hair. Laughing excitedly, the children pluck blindly, and you admonish them, "That's enough, we'd better go in!"

For the rain has joined the wind in rollicking attack. It comes pelting, cool and tingling on the faces of flowers and children alike as, dropping things and darting back for them, you scurry back into the house.

"Well, now we've got work to do. Jimmy, you're the best climber, you can get up to the top shelf and bring the vases down."

"It's like a party," somebody says. "The house will be all dressed up for a party!" And that's the way it feels—festive and gay and dancing with color, as outside the window the rains come down.

How Feminine Are the Trees

The porch is strewn with petals and wisps and furrings, as if the trees too are cleaning house. . . .

The pines lift their little yellow candles, unearthed from long storage in winter closets. The candlesticks have been polished. They look pert and crisp and ready to entertain. . . .

The maples and poplars and elms drip a frail pink froth. Or they trail beady little pendants, bright wind-tossed fringes, in a kind of Victorian opulence and nicety. . . .

The dogwoods are like a host of girls in graduation dresses, huddled in white clusters among the rest. Up close their white blossoms are lifted on hands that seem suppliant, palms up, to spread before you their exquisite offering of waxy blooms. . . .

The trees are feminine. Strong yet dainty. They dress like women, sway like women, whisper and chat like women. Keep house like women, performing their exquisitely feminine tasks.

Paper Towers

How beautiful is a back porch piled with papers. Yes, papers. And magazines in a dizzy heap. . . . Come quickly, oh come quickly all ye Scouts and rescue workers; rescue me from this accumulation.

For printed matter multiplies to some awful inundation. Like the porridge in the "Sorcerer's Apprentice" it would engulf you if you didn't sometimes turn it off. It would possess not only the whole house but the porch, the driveway, the street.

But meanwhile the stacks of it stand tall, catching the morning light. The pages still shine. There are bits and tags of the artists' colors still thrusting out like little flowers struggling to bloom. And the newspapers lie mute, thick and dove-grey in feeling, richly resigned.

There is something sad and wonderful about all the treasury of words, read and unread, that they contain.

A part of you feels guilty, vaguely troubled at what you know you've missed. You long to delay their disappearance, to draw them back.

But no, once you weaken you'll be sitting on the steps all morning, sorting and re-sorting, and only lug too many back in. But, at least, you can send out to them a kind of apology for their abandonment.

Meanwhile, there is a subtle loveliness about these paper towers. One pile reposes on a porch chair—like a mother holding them on her lap, her strong metal arms around them. The homely charm of this picture is curiously comforting.

Goodbye, all you magazines and newspapers. Thanks for the hours of pleasure I found in you. I'm sorry I have to neglect even one of you. You are still beautiful awaiting your fate here at my back door.

The Month of Miracles

May is the month of miracles. The white locks of winter have broken. April's glassy rains have wakened the trembling life in the earth, and the sun now leads it forth like a proud bridegroom.

Fields and woodside ring with birdsong, wild flowers run rife, and forsythia's golden fountains lend their splendor to the humblest yard.

May is discovery, May is wonder. It is children crying, enchanted, "Look, look, violets!" and crouching with grubby fingers to pluck the elusive hideaways, leaving the stems too short.

It is robins learning to fly, and baby squirrels. And when they fall, it is rescue squads of little folks tenderly carting them home to Mother, who can heal and save anything, they believe.

May is planting and planning. It is the smell of paint as Mother decides to touch up the porch swing; and the smell of new-turned earth as Dad digs in the garden. It is children begging to "help" as you set out plants, or pleading even more passionately for a garden patch of their own. It is noses pressed anxiously to the kitchen window, and faithful trips out back each day until the triumphant cry rings out, "Look, look, it's up!" before the thrilling spectacle of a wobbly green trail to mark the miracle, like a thread of tiny beads.

May is memories. The fragrance of sun on the grass, of lilacs, bring them flooding back: Past and popcorn and ruffled crepe paper, and the scurry of feet in the dusk as May baskets were hung. The white shoes you simply had to have for the Maypole winding, and the delicious suspense over who would be chosen queen.

May is a time of festival—for bird and child and flower and tree. And for the heart.

Fishing While Reading Poe

You sit on the dock one morning, presumably fishing, but primarily reading Poe's "Eleanora," known also as "The Valley of the Many-Colored Grass."

The sky is slate-colored. The lake a glassy gunmetal, gold-plated along the edges, with the overlapping reflections of gray-green, gold-green willow trees.

Clouds, like restless ghosts, begin to haunt the water, to prowl the sky. Raindrops fall, splattering your book. Each draws a circle as it strikes, and within each little center is a tiny crystal bead. . . .

"And here and there, in groves about this grass, like wilderness of dreams, sprang up fantastic trees," you read, "whose tall slender stems stood not upright, but slanted gracefully toward the light that peered at noon-day into the center of the valley——"

Each time you become absorbed in the liquid music of Poe's words, a bobber begins a frantic dance. You clap shut the book and rush to attendance, only to draw up an empty hook.

You rebait it. From a handy thermos jug, replenish the coffee you've been sipping, spilled in your haste. Try to find your place in the book:

"The golden and silver fish haunted the river, out of the bosom of which issued, little by little, a mur-

mur that swelled, at length, into a lulling melody more divine than that of the harp of Aeolus—"

Wham! The golden and silver fish that haunt your lake are clever. Away goes another one with your line. And by the time you're frantically trying to pull it in, with a taunting flip of tail, it has escaped.

Distress wars with a sense of some amused, dreamy awareness of harmony and fate. It is one of those lovely, cloudy mornings when you too are adrift in a misty valley of many-colored grass.

The May Basket

The world is like a vast May basket hung on your own front door. As if dull gray winter simply disappeared while you slept. . . . And lo, on waking, you find all this loveliness.

Forsythia in gay and golden fountains. . . . The azaleas, so lush and richly colored they look almost edible. . . . Dogwoods bursting white and fragile as china cups. . . . Wisteria trailing its lavender lace over old houses (the houses must be very old to receive this perennial embrace), or roving wild over weathered fences and ancient trees. . . . Tulips opening their pointed lips. . . .

These flowers and so many spilling over the very top of the basket to be admired. While at its bottom, tucked daintily among the leaves, are the violets, the fragrant lilies of the valley, the pert primroses. They are like children hiding, small and secret, almost giggling.

The primroses, particularly. Eager little flowers who come early to spring's party, yet somewhat retiring, for they hold back a bit, loving the shade. (How strange that the old phrase "the primrose path" means something dashing and forbidden. The little flowers would be shocked if they knew; they would consult each other, amused and dismayed.)

The world each day is almost too beautiful to be believed. It's like a huge May basket arranged for your admiration and left on your doorstep.

Magic Under Foot

Newly laid kitchen flooring, bright and smooth and shining, its pattern echoing the gay colors of your curtains, the copperware on the wall, and the ivy spilling from a pot upon the window sill. . . .

The pleasure of sweeping that floor the first few times. The broom glides smoothly over its surface, like a dancer practicing pirouettes and jetes. The broom dips spryly into corners, routing out crumbs and dirt and scooting them into a pile where they cannot hide away. . . .

"Let me help, let me sweep!" small would-be aides implore. And you give the time-honored answer of mothers, "All right, honey, you can hold the dustpan."

And one of them squats, gets an earnest grip on the yellow handle, while you patiently strive to hit the target which is always too high or too low or "all sidewise and bias" as my own mother used to laugh.

Yet in a minute the task is done and you stand regarding it a second longer, this shining and cheery expanse. And you think—how strange, that spirits can get such a lift from so basic and everyday an object as simply bright new unmarred kitchen flooring beneath your feet.

You hang the broom on its usual hook in the

closet and close the door. With a quick cautious glance to make sure nobody's watching, you fling your arms in a joyous gesture; suddenly YOU become the dancer practicing jetes and pirouettes!

Lilac Time

Lilacs nodding over your neighbor's fence arouse a whole host of nostalgic associations. They are like the ostrich plumes elegant ladies used to wear on their hats, tall and frail and grandly swaying, as their wearers sang the hymns in church, or bowed their heads in prayer . . .

The lilacs themselves are as old-fashioned as the sachets women used to make out of satin and fill with perfumed powder and tuck beneath their corset covers.

As charming and eternally lovely as the fragile white-haired mistress of this domed and cupolaed house where the lilacs choke the path . . .

She comes out, where you stand drinking in their moist sweetness on this bright spring morning. "We set them out when I was a bride," she says. "Lilacs take years to develop." Reaching up, she breaks off a branch, sniffs it, reminiscently smiling, and bestows it upon you. "Help yourself, take all you want."

You too reach up, draw a shower of fragrant, trembling plumes into your arms. You carry their lavender-loveliness into the house, arrange them in your tallest vases.

They crown the mantel, they admire themselves in the mirror above the hall table. Their perfume fills the rooms. They are like gracious, plumed and sacheted ladies come for a party!

Maytime Morning

Still in his pajamas and slippers, your toddler sits on the steps with you, watching the older ones off to school.

Other youngsters pass, carrying books and lunch boxes. The morning air is cool and sweet as wine.

The trees are in full leaf now and greener than green in this early time of day, winking with dew like the grasses. They speak, a pleasant yet somehow urgent whispering. And from all the trees the birds call, their voices like bells in a carillon.

Your little one points up delightedly, his voice as musical as the birds as he tries to imitate their chirping songs.

There is a nest of blackbirds in the hollow of a tree that bends before the door. The mother keeps vigil from a higher branch while the father carries worms and twigs and bits of string. Now and then you see black heads lift, yellow beaks yawn wide.

You are reluctant to go in. You cross the broad, shining lawn, which smells so sweet from last night's cutting.

You study the garden with that perennial feeling of hope, wonder and faint anxiety. How slowly it changes. Yet every new sign of life is a kind of personal reassurance. As if that mute pact that is made between root and seed, earth and human being, is to be honored, so fear not.

The roses? Yes, three of the new ones are sending forth delicate ruffled shoots. Two still crouch there, stubbornly barren, and you scrape back a little more of the wax in which they came.

The older bushes, however, are laden with great swollen buds that will burst any minute; strips of red and yellow can be seen through their shells.

The peony bushes are fat and laden, too, their buds round and hard as marbles, in contrast to the slim ellipses of the rosebuds. Lush and regal as orchids, the irises are already in bloom.

"Fower!" You stifle a cry of protest as the little fellow snaps off the head of your largest, loveliest one. Proudly he toddles up, face shining, the treasure held out in both fists. "Fower for Mommy."

"Why, thank you, honey." You snatch him up and hold him close.

The Fragrances of Spring

Rain. Soft on the face, cool on the cheek, and drawing such fragrances out of all it touches—earth, grass, flowers, leaves. Even pavements, rooftops, the feathers of birds or the flanks of dog or cat. All smell different, revitalized, somehow life-eager after spring rain. . . . And the rain itself, it has a refreshing near-fragrance all its own. So new, so utterly clean.

Flowers. How delicate the combination of their perfumes in the spring. Apple and cherry blossoms, lilacs, wild clover, the first roses. Those with more subtle scents or no smell at all—azaleas, dogwood, forsythia, some irises—even these emit a lovely essence that joins the general blend.

And the grass, the tender new grass, especially sweet when freshly cut. And the earth itself, teeming with vitality seen and unseen—worms and buds and sprouting seeds.

Spring stirs all this up for us, sun-warms it, rain-sweetens it, wind-tosses it, brews for us a subtle but heady perfume no mortals could match. All we can do is breathe it into our beings, rejoicing that the Creator gives us this extra dimension of beauty, the fragrances of spring.

Summer

Daisies

How dainty is a daisy.

What a fragile and lovely splattering of white petals encircling a heart of gold. A daisy is a lesson in simplicity. It is like an exquisite woman, tall, slender, plain. Yet beautiful in her very lack of adornment.

Like the Mona Lisa, her elusive charm etches itself upon the memory. She is spare yet precious. "Daisies don't tell" either. And it is this quality of something secret, something ordinary yet rare that gives the daisy its special quality.

Daisies, big shasta daisies, are blooming on the patio and in the garden. I can see their pristine faces as I breakfast on the balcony. They are looking up with a faintly imagined smile upon their petaled countenances. And a horde of wild daisies romp just beyond—along the lake bank, peeping stubbornly from the rocky hillside, starring distant meadows.

They are smaller, fragile looking echoes of the carefully nurtured occupants of the garden. Yet how tough these strangers are. How they multiply and survive! Sun and storm do not faze them, nor preying insects. Unlike their short-lived sisters, these hardy cousins last.

I have often brought them home in buckets and set them out urging, "Welcome, now stay here!" But they are unpredictable for all their tough nature. Here they peep, there they cluster, but mostly they simply vanish—only to pop up when you're not looking, in some totally unlikely spot.

No matter. There is nothing like the sight of daisies on a hot summer morning to refresh the spirits, soothe the soul, untangle the complexities of life. Just to see them is to be reminded that on this crowded and often difficult planet there are still innocent simple things—like daisies.

Children Were Born to Love Flowers

Children were born to love flowers.

Does it begin in the hospital, I wonder, when their mothers are surrounded by bouquets to mark their advent into the world? Does the new baby somehow absorb their scent, their bright colors, and thereafter associate them with happy occasions?

But no, though a child be born in the remotest places, far from such an experience, almost before he can walk he is awakening to the joy that strikes the human heart from that fragile thing, a flower.

A flower! He rushes toward it on still unsteady feet and claims it for his own. He plunges his face into it to drink deep of its fragrance, feel the velvet of its petals. Then too often comes the rude awakening, "No, no!" And it is wrested from him. Sometimes the hands are spanked. "Naughty hands. You mustn't pick the flower."

For he's ruined it, of course. It is crushed now. Limp. A broken, stemless head, his lovely flower.

Yet children are not easily denied this native rapport with blooming things. And they are not choosy about a flower's pedigree. To a child a dandelion is quite as enchanting as a prize-winning rose. They rush to squat among the prodigal patches to pluck stubby bouquets for mother. They wail when dads attack their favorites with trowels or mowers.

When they are old enough they braid them into garlands. To children dandelions are treasures, as precious as gold.

And clover, wild clover with its sweet perfume. . . . And violets hiding daintily in unexpected places, so that to find them is high adventure.

And to be given packets of seed and allowed to plant flowers of their own. That is even better, for it is to have a hand in creating this marvel, a flower. They beg it of you—some little patch of ground by garage or fence or garbage pail. And it is precious to them, they haunt it, hover over it, and when the first wobbly touch of green appears, are ecstatic. The miracle is beginning. They guard it jealously against intruders. And woe betide any careless creature, human or animal, that steps upon "my flowers."

Some flowers seem especially designed for children. Children love pansies and bring them to you to arrange, with the little monkey faces peering over the rim of the bowl.

Youngsters love marigolds too, and nasturtiums —their bright colors and tangy scent. Snowballs are a favorite, reminding them of winter games. (Watch out lest a snowball fight ensue in the yard in June. Nobody gets hurt but the mess is mighty, and the place looks as if a summer blizzard has struck.)

And children love the old-fashioned flowers that few people seem to raise any more. Bleeding hearts, like tiny gemmed valentines. And hollyhocks, which can be made into dolls if an adult shows how. And snapdragons, which can be popped.

Curiously, as we grow up so do our feelings

about certain flowers. A gardenia, white, waxy and unutterably fragrant, is usually the first flower pinned on a young girl's shoulder for a prom. Roses signify developing romance—a sweetheart sends them, long-stemmed, in a box. When she becomes the bride she wears an orchid for luncheons in her honor or as she leaves on her honeymoon.

The little girl who plucked the dandelions, the short-stemmed pansies and braided the delicate clover, is grown.

Some flowers seem especially designed for children.

Sights of a Summer Morning

Hollyhocks nodding delicately over your neighbor's fence, like young ladies returned from some prim Victorian era in their ruffled bonnets, delighted to be here in modern suburbia, but about to gasp and giggle and throw up leaf-gloved hands in surprise.

A robin taking his morning ablutions in the puddle left by a hose that has dribbled all night. His saucy flutterings and peckings and dippings—then away he wings with a song in his throat.

Two little girls playing "tent" by hiding in the blankets a mother is sunning on the line.

Armada for Breakfast

Sitting on the dock one morning, idly fishing, you hear the approaching ducks. Around the bend where your husband stands casting, they glide, a merry armada, sending forth greetings.

Usually visiting in twos or threes, this time they have joined forces: Five snow-white ones, a browny-gray youngster, and a big jaunty slate colored goose. "Honk, honk—quaawk, quaawk!"

"We're being invaded, and they sound hungry. Better get some bread."

Securing fishing rods with rocks, you scurry up the steps. "Get up," you call a daughter. "We've got company for breakfast!"

She trails you sleepily, hair in her eyes, pajamas crumpled, but delightfully displaying the usual just-awake grumpiness. "Oh, look, lookit the little one! But he isn't getting any." She stands hurling the crumbs and crusts. However, he scurries and dips, the selfish elders beat him. "Come on, honey, over here."

Luring him with a special piece, she gets him aside. Greedily he snatches, downs it. The others circle excitedly about, thrashing and crowding each other, like people to whom money is being tossed. Frantically they emit their inelegant cries. Your daughter notes, "They don't really quack, they croak! They sound like engines that need oiling."

Quivering with excitement, the Dalmatian stands on the dock. Because of her the ducks keep their distance. But the crumbs that fall close attract the bluegills. Up they dart, flirting shadows of silver, to snatch the crumbs with little popping sounds.

When at last the sack is empty, the ducks coast off, discussing it in voices more subdued, satisfied. Yet before leaving, they circle and maneuver about, drawing their beautiful patterns of reflections.

"They're thanking us," the little girl says. "They're doing a goodbye dance."

"We should thank them," you say, as the bluegills continue their impudent nosing. "Now maybe we'll catch some fish!"

The Noble Brick

What a beautiful thing is a brick!

Rosy red with newness, or pale pink with age, a brick is one of the finest things ever devised by man.

Hold a brick in your hand a moment; feel its sturdy weight, hard yet with a surface softness. And if it is an old brick dusted with a delicate bloom, like the cheeks of an elderly person grown gentle and wise with age.

A brick is truly elemental. Out of the earth itself it comes, to be molded and then baked in the fire. Joined by mortar to its brothers, it serves man in old and infinite ways, building his walls, his fences, his schools, his churches, his houses and the patios he is inspired to lay in his backyard.

The life of a brick is long. It endures thus sometimes for centuries. And often when its time of service is finished in one direction and walls come tumbling down, the brick is rescued, carted away by truck to have the dried ligaments of mortar beaten away, its surface cleaned, and given new existence in the form of new churches and walls and homes.

A brick has a homely humor. A brick chuckles as it tumbles with its kind into your vacant lot. As if the bricks were laughing at the spectacle of the human family forever about its business of building and tearing down. Yet, in a kindly way, making a sturdy music in the morning of man's vision of the house or the wall or the patio he is fashioning.

A brick has character. A brick has beauty and quality and grace. That's why we say of a person with such attributes, "He's a brick." To be a brick is to be a noble thing.

Radiance

The lake has unfurled its flags. The wind provides the stripes of light and shade, the sun its living stars.

They leap, flash, die and are continually reborn. Each is a perfect five-pointed thing. They wink and blaze ceaselessly on the rippling silver-blue banners.

And watching them you wonder: Why does man love radiance so much? From infancy he is attracted by anything that shines. Toys and baubles, sequins and spangles, jewels and silver and gold.

Yet why? Why not the shadows, the darkness, the deep sweet peaceful lack of light? Is it because the sun is the source of life? Warming us by day, drawing forth from the earth almost everything that we need to survive.

And then, in its lavishness, tossing us all this brilliance besides. Making leaves and grasses shine, joining forces with the wind to scatter fiery flags across a lake.

The sun is in league even with the moon when the day has gone, still silvering the waters, both of them. The very stars, distant and mysterious though they are, beckon to us—because they are the many little suns of night.

How Gently They Come to You

You sit on the dock feeding dry bread to the bluegills. They come swarming up in frantic swirls. They dart to the surface and snatch a crumb and dive away. Their bodies are gray-green shadows, or catching a shaft of light, iridescent gold and blue. Mysterious living creatures, greed propelled, alert yet wary, coasting about awaiting the precise instant when all may be risked for a fragment of food.

A young turtle comes paddling up to see what's going on like a curious, shy adolescent, who, not sure he dares come to the party, hovers apart. You toss him a crust, but the fish are faster. It's vanished before his eager maneuvers reach the prize. You throw him another; this time the jutting head is quick. With a kind of awkward, comical grace, he sinks hastily down before he can be robbed.

You sit feeding the fish and turtle. And think— I could catch them. With this bait or some other I could entice them to me and carry some of them away. How nice not to want to. To just be giving to them and enjoying them instead.

You scatter the last crumbs onto the water and when they are finally gone, the whole miniature company goes too. It is all they wanted of you. But as you sit quietly soaking up the sun, other creatures begin gently to come to you.

An orange caterpillar undulates across your ankle, fat and furry, like a little old lady hastening to a party, swathed in her stole. Where is she bound with such almost gay urgency? What is her business? Dragonflies hover, slender aircraft. Butterfly paint-blue at head and tail. A huge bee drones over your head. Still, sit very still, it is only wondering what strange tumbled flower this may be, what nectar lurks there. A butterfly lands on your toe— large and velvety, robed in a silken purple; you are for the moment its pedestal. Two tiny, almost invisible toads hop across the wood, small boys chasing each other. Finally, and most thrilling, a pair of wild canaries carry on their courtship in the tangle of wild roses but an arm's length away.

There is no fear, no separation, so long as you sit quietly. Nature accepts you, merges with you, asking nothing. Nature brings its peace and loveliness to you.

Fire on the Beach

The moon is a pale golden melon half in a lavender sky.

The fire on the beach lifts golden tongues from a rosy heart. You hear it snapping and crackling, along with the voices of the young people who are laughing and kidding, and the music of a transistor radio that they have hung from a tree branch.

They have built their fire in the space between two rearing rocks. The rocks rise behind and about them, placid, ancient and serene, their sides illuminated by the fire like the sides of a cave.

"They won't let us come, they won't let us roast marshmallows with them!" the smaller fry complain to you, where you sit with friends on the patio just above. "Can we build our own fire? Can we have a bonfire too?"

"Sure, why not?" you say. "If you'll gather the wood."

Now you see these other figures, sprite-small in the moon and the firelight, prowling about, gathering up twigs and leafy sticks. You watch them crouching over their pitiful pile of paper and inadequate fuel, striking matches that only go out—especially when they get scared and drop them. So your husband rises and goes down to help. He gathers an armload, and over their protests, "Let us do it, we know how!" gets their fire laid.

Two bonfires now are leaping on the sands below, snapping and calling to each other and waving white arms of smoke.

"Whew! That surely should be enough to keep the bugs away," someone laughs. "But doesn't it smell good?"

There is the acrid tang of burning wood, the fishy smell of the water, the odor of leaf mold and earth. The moon, looking cool and almost succulent in the sky, seems—like happiness—close enough to hold in your hands.

Alone with Loveliness

The lake is a flat black mirror, shining and smooth. You slip away after dinner, and cautiously untie the canoe, undiscovered and unshouted at by family, unfollowed even by the dog.

Carefully, carefully, almost holding your breath, you push away from the dock and glide across the still expanse.

Nobody has missed you yet—move swiftly, dip the paddle fast . . . sweep the liquid distance between you. If they want to catch you now they'll have to swim!

You are alone with loveliness, overhead and below. The last clouds lingering after the sunset are mirrored on the water. And even stronger reflections fall from rocks and docks and leaning trees. Each is imprinted as clearly as a picture from a negative. It is almost impossible to tell where water ceases and rocks and trees and sky begin.

In this picture you move, melting, blending, merging, too. You can see your own reflection lifting the paddle, and hear the motion as a gliding, half-silent, half-conscious thing. It is as if you are moving across a magical ballroom floor, polished as smooth as marble, yet soft, soft and silken, as in a dream.

Night things begin to chirr and clack and shrill and jingle their tiny bells and castanets in the thickets and marshes and trees. Fireflies begin to dip, bright sparks that the water faithfully duplicates. And your spirit joins their secret chorus. You are alone with loveliness.

Summer Treasures

Summer is a time for treasures. Especially for bright-eyed children who go discovering.

Dandelions are not weeds; they are golden coins flung about by a lavish hand. And how many things you can do with dandelions! You can pluck them for fat bouquets for playhouses and mothers (although they don't last long). You can braid them into heavy bracelets and necklaces. You can wear them for rings. When a dandelion is budding it looks like a lady's huge solitaire in a tiffany setting; pick it and twine it about your finger. When a dandelion has gone to seed it's a puffy balloon, a lovely thing for blowing. Blow hard, blow hard and watch its delicate fronds float away. Then what have you left? A pearl, a round white pearl. This too you can wear as a ring by winding its stem.

Clover is lovely too for adorning. Pick it as long-stemmed as you can on a summer's day when the world is sleepy-humming, and braid it into chains. A mother or older sister will show you how to fasten new blossoms into the strands. Work hard and soon you will have enough for a bracelet, a necklace, a belt, a crown! Clover smells sweet, especially when the sun is hot and the mourning doves croon.

Buttercups are very useful. Hold them under

somebody's chin and see if there's a golden shadow; if so, he or she likes butter. Daisies aren't supposed to tell—but if you have a secret sweetheart they will. Just pick off the petals one by one chanting "He loves me, he loves me not," and you'll have your answer.

Hollyhocks are old-fashioned flowers marvelous for making dolls. Turn a blossom upside down and you have a tiny lady in a ruffled organdy skirt. Snapdragons pop if you press them—look out, they might bite you. Jack-in-the-pulpit is a funny little guy who's trying to tell you something. Put your ear down to him, listen—what is it?

Four leaf clovers are lucky. Hunt in the patch long enough and if you find one, wear it in your shoe. Sometimes there are whole patches of four leaf clovers. They will bring you marvelous luck—you can give them away or sell them to friends for a penny; but if you tell friends where they are—well, you may not be so lucky.

But the luckiest thing about being small in summer is being close enough to the earth and all living things to see how beautiful they are. How many priceless purposes they can be used for but how few adults realize it.

That is, unless they remember.

Summer Storm

How glorious is an unexpected storm. Especially when the day has been muggy, heat-weighted, with no promise in the burning sky.

"If only it would rain," people say, scanning that heavy brightness. And suddenly, strangely out of nowhere, it is as if a soft dark veil is being drawn. Rain is in the newly quickened air—you can feel it, smell it. And the wind, like a slumbering giant that has wakened and must be about his business, springs up and goes tearing across roads and yards and fields.

And with it, people begin scampering all directions to cars and houses, seeking shelter.

But the rain is too swift. It suddenly comes pelting, as if a giant switch had been turned on.

You roll back porch rugs, move furniture and stand watching. The rain moves in a mad and merry invasion. First, on that sleek, uneasy surface, comes a silvery bombardment. A hail of little bullets that explode in puffs of smoke. Then, wind propelled, an army's swift assault.

While nearer, on the tracked and dusty walkway, drops spatter like fat and vigorous elves stamping up and down.

You say: "I wish those little people carried brooms and could sweep that walkway while they're at it."

On the porch swing, a child sits pensive, chin in hand. "Oh, you and your little people, Mom! To me the rain is like a lady dancing. I don't know why—but she's all cold and silvery and she wears a dress trimmed with crystal beads."

"She does!" you exclaim. For now you too see the beads sparkling on the world's swaying chiffon gown. They pour from the trees, cling to the porch's old dark screen.

Then suddenly it is over. The skies lighten. The armies in furious battle retreat. The little people dissolve into puddles that catch the returning sun. Beads still cling to the screen and drip musically from the trees, but the misty gown is gone.

Yawning and stretching, the wind goes back to finish a nap. The grass sparkles, the frogs resume their chorus in the marsh, the birds rejoice. The sluggish, grubby, heat-weary world—refreshed from its bath—begins to prate and sing.

The Couple in the Trees

Nature offers us a continuous game of picture puzzles. Every child loves to find likenesses in the clouds.

"See the parade! The circus parade. There goes the elephant—see his trunk, and right behind him there's a bareback rider.

". . . Oh, its changing, look, look the elephant's trunk has turned into a long pink scarf and the bareback lady's reaching for it."

Few of us ever outgrow this entrancing entertainment. Almost without thinking, our eyes stray skyward, seeking and finding images. Not only in the ever-changing shapes of clouds, but often in the trees.

Just up the hill at our home the trees rise thick and green. Their tops brush the sky at a fairly uniform range. But several reach higher than the rest. And years ago two in particular became for me a young couple. A young wife leaning toward her husband fixing his tie. Every time I sat on the patio there they were, always in this human situation.

And gradually, over the years, they thickened, even as people do. His chin, and hers, doubled. His hair became a bit tousled, hers acquired a bun. I began to notice that he had his mouth open, as if to discuss (perhaps protest?) her ministrations. And

76

sometimes when the wind blew, it was as if her hand moved to pat him or maybe shake her finger.

Each time I return I look up to make sure they are still there. A much older couple now, grown closer in their thickness, almost merged. Yet still facing each other in some eternal attitude of caring. Of wifely attention and male submission, secretly pleased.

How dear they have become, how real they are, these people of trees.

Life Can Be a Painting

All life can be a painting if you but see it so. A gray day, for instance, when you go to pick out plumbing fixtures with your husband—which sounds like an uninspiring enterprise. And yet— what pleasure to wander about the spacious open lot peering into the crates where tubs are upended, black bottoms looking rather jaunty, with only glimpses of their colors to whet the eye. Sunshine-yellow, deep slate blue, olive-green, rosy beige.

Or to enter the huge skylit warehouse and linger before the lovely displays, in a sweet torment of indecision. And to drink hot coffee from the big friendly urn while males consult at counters, with much maneuvering of figures and workmen's tape measures, much jargon of pipes and fittings.

And feeling superfluous (having finally cast your vote for the blue) to return to the car for some music and a magazine. . . . And yet to be aware of the curious beauty all about. As if even so utilitarian a place has become part of a giant painting. The clean slender dignity of the building, its aluminum siding a pleasant shade of mauve against the pearl-gray sky. While in its yard stands an enormous mustard-yellow machine of some kind, with giant wheels and long yellow arms reaching their bright obliques into space, as if to embrace the world. And its brilliant yellow is echoed by the gaudy mustard flowers blowing in nearby fields.

Rimming the yard are steel fences, silver-meshed, and beside them stacks of rust-colored pipes, like logs from some steel forest. And bending above them are two workmen in faded blue jeans, moving with the unconscious grace of bluebirds, while overhead the clouds part and streaks of the same blue shine through.

In the foreground march the bleached wooden crates, with only their hints and glimpses of color, row on row. And cutting across this composition fine black power lines go looping and blackbirds skim. While a small yellow warbler perches singing on a nearby post.

And all this is a huge and private painting. A silent not-quite-still life held up to be admired in its steely frame of fence.

Fourth of July

Half of the fun of the Fourth is when you are driving through the country and your husband yields to the children's clamoring and stops at a roadside fireworks stand. . . .

The sunlight slants through the trees where birds are singing, and illuminates the already shining faces of your young as they spill out. . . .

Perspiring, public-spirited men and boys behind the counter welcome you heartily and explain, "Howdy, folks, we're raising money to send kids to camp." . . .

Purses are produced, and after much weighing and choosing, big rattling sacks are filled with the gaudy and thrilling loot—sparklers, pinwheels and snakes. . . .

Your husband buys some extra sparklers. "For spares, in case the neighbors come down. And how many fountains and helicopters do you think—?" . . . .

While you're about it, you stroll across trampled, sweet smelling pasture grass, and from a tiny lady in a sunbonnet buy huge red strawberries and country eggs and an enormous green whale of a watermelon floating in an icy tub. . . .

"Well, everybody got everything they need now

for the Fourth?" the head of the household asks, locking the back of the car. And filled with contentment and a tingling anticipation, you set off down the highway toward home.

Morning Mist

The mists have come in the night. You wake to find them draping the world outside your windows. At the lake they are a blind tremulous wall between you and the trees on the opposite shore. They rise from the waters below the cabin in a gentle, enticing mystery. You can hear the birds calling through them . . . with a note of gaiety and urgency, somehow.

Calling to each other, or to you? Their chirps and flutings are sharpened by the very softness through which they spurt. "Where are you?" the birdsongs seem to be asking. "Come find us!"

You slip into a suit, and start down the moist rock steps to the water. "It's too foggy—you'll get lost!" somebody warns from a window. But you tiptoe through the hazy whiteness. The dark dripping branches of trees bend above you, protectively. The light shimmers through. . . . No blind pilgrimage this, rather a secret exploration.

The float emerges, a broad rectangle before you, and it is like stepping onto a stage. For all around, like huge backdrops painted by some mystical genius, rise the muffled shapes and masses of the trees. And here on the float, bedecking boat and ladder and upended canoe, is a jolly fretwork of cobwebbing.

White and shimmering—hammocks and doilies and nets for circuses.

It is all too exquisite not to share. Like the birds, you too start calling: "Come on! Come on, get up you sleepyheads, come see!" Only one voice responds, one face at the window, yawning, grimacing, nodding in drowsy agreement before going back to bed.

Oh well. . . . You plunge into the smoking water that is cold and smooth and soft as the mists all about. Stroke through its silkiness . . . turn on your back and float.

On the banks wild yellow foxglove and burning fires of butterfly weed are the only spears of color, thrusting through. While the mists hover all about you . . . and the great mysterious shapes of dimly sensed massed trees.

It is like floating in the landscape of a dream. It is as if you too had been transformed, disembodied, become one with the silent shining mists . . . floating in the very pulse of eternity.

Name Tags, Please

How sad it is not to know the names of things.

A name is so important to all our relationships. A baby doesn't really become a person until the certificate has been signed and he officially bears a name. The people we encounter at parties and meetings— there is always a sense of strangeness, vague discomfort until we are introduced. And we all undergo the misery of meeting someone who seems to know us intimately, and of searching wildly for his name.

In a small way this is true with things in the world of nature. How many dear, delightful little people in the plant world we would enjoy so much more if only we knew their names.

For instance, one day on a walk in the woods we came upon some clumps of low, lovely parasol-shaped leaves. They bowed to us as if in greeting, and we paused and bowed back to them. Then we knelt to become better acquainted, and found them two-toned, their large down-curved leaves mottled with a deeper purpley green.

"What do you suppose they are?" We all conferred; and one of the children said whimsically, "If only there was somebody to introduce us—say if the wind or the sun could talk, or maybe a bird that happened to be friends of theirs."

Bemused, oddly frustrated, we plucked a few and

brought them along to look up in a book somewhere.

And as we later picnicked on a blanket on the grass we felt the same teasing puzzlement. For all about there was a lively little flirtation of delicate unknown flowers. Tiny white starrings of petals exquisitely made; infinitely like lady's slippers, except that they were so wee, "They'd have to be fairy slippers instead!" one of the youngsters exclaimed.

"Maybe they're lily-putians," grinned a son.

Violets—these we all know, and the bold shaggy dandelions, and the sweet smelling wild clover; but oh, the delicate, fragile wonder-world of anonymous country sproutings and leafings and bloomings that seem to plead, "Hi, let's get acquainted," but are helpless to vouchsafe their own little names.

Then there are those permanent guests in your own yard, the trees. How many years they have stood there, providing a home for the birds that waken you in the morning, a strong arm for the swing; shading you from the sun and sharing their wealth (and work) of brilliant leaves—yet otherwise ignored, anonymous.

The sturdy oaks—grandfatherly old fellows, we know them so well we take them for granted. And of course the trusty maples, the cottonwoods, and the blossoming ones like dogwoods and mimosas—they proclaim their identity through leaf and fruit and flower. Yet how shamefully neglected stand so many others equally faithful, equally attractive, like patient people at a party unrecognized by their very host. This remissness I have vowed to correct. I've gotten out an old tree book (souvenir of my husband's boyhood—thank goodness growing things don't go out of date), and resolved to make them welcome after all this time, to greet them properly, every blessed one—by name!

When Ducks Come Calling

The ducks come coasting down the creek in their bland, unhurried glide.

They are whiter than white, they are shimmering in the sunlight. Their feathers are a silken sculpturing, padding the curved elegance of their backs.

They propel themselves with their yellow feet, effortlessly, then trail them like half-folded fans.

They quack and quarrel and mate with a wild splashing and fluttering of wings, then proceed as peacefully as before.

One or two stand on the bank loafing, or pecking at the sand with their round flat bills.

There is a lovely gray one, its wings blending in bits of blue, violet, green; its bill a mottled agate color.

They probe their own necks with their bills. They waddle a few steps and sink into the water, proceeding toward the rocks on the opposite side.

The children go wild when they see them coming. "Ducks, duck! Give us some bread for the ducks!" they cry.

And they race madly to the bank, clutching the little sacks of bread that you have saved. They fling the bread and shriek to see the gluttonous scramble, and diving and somersaulting. They frantically beg for more. And when the bread supply is exhausted

and the ducks glide off, they stand with faces for-
lorn.

"Ducks, duck, duck—come back, ducks!" then
futilely implore. "Oh well, let 'em go. No manners!"

Beauty on Horseback

The horses are saddled, and the farmer leads, a gentle man with seamed brown skin and pale blue eyes. The horses are all three the rich color of mahogany; their flanks and great hips gleam.

They keep tossing their heads against the flies, and the old-timer they've decided is best for you snatches a mouthful of grass when she can.

Across the pasture you ride, the horse's flesh warm beneath your knees. Daisies star the hillside, and there is a gold matting of tiny yellow weeds. The earth is lavender, the fence a weathered gray.

The farmer leans down to close the gate and you proceed up the gravel road.

Your daughter's younger, friskier mount trots by and then gallops far ahead; but for your sake the farmer keeps to a steadier pace.

He turns in the saddle, sitting sidewise, chewing on his pipe and gesturing to neighboring sights. "That's a binder—they're haying yonder." (His own barn is already filled with gray prickly rectangles of new-mown hay giving off its idyllic perfume.) "Let's go up to the house."

Dogs come baying out to greet you, but the white house, choked with roses on the hillside, is still. "They're not home, but we can visit their steers."

One horse shies at the red beasts blandly chewing beside the fence; the others halt and match the cattle's bold and vacant stares. "They're Herefords," the farmer informs you.

Back down the road, hooves rattle the pebbles, wild roses and honeysuckle fight the fence for space. Their mingled perfumes fill the air. Then off along another hidden little roadway.

Hooves plop in yellow puddles, skirls of water fly. Then you can feel the great muscles straining as sure feet pick their way up a ferny bank and along a narrow trail.

Ahead is a little sparkling stream; a spring spills out of a mossy, rock-clotted hillside.

The horses cross the water, so clear you see the minnows darting; they climb the opposite bank up to their hooves in a thick mattress of damp, silver-gold leaves.

You are in an enchanted forest! Light bangles and flashes, rains down in freckling showers; it threads and laces through the slender trunks. Birds dip and dart and run their liquid scales. The air is pure and cold and sparkling like the stream.

You cannot drink it deeply enough, that air with its heady fragrance of leaf and earth and flower. It is a heady elixir, more potent than wine. "Oh, if only you could bottle that air and take some of it back to town!"

"Well, I've got a good air compressor," the farmer laughs. He pauses to tap his pipe against a stump. "Maybe we could go into business. Bet it'd fetch a pretty price."

The High Heeled Pigs

The pigs go stilting along like fat little old ladies balancing themselves gracefully on high heels. When the children call to them in young eager voices in imitation of the farmer, they come foolishly banging and bunting at each other to reach the food they expect. In disappointment, they snuff and snort along the ground and crunch grudgingly and incessantly at the old scattered kernels of corn. They are monstrously fat and lazy, especially the great pink sows that lie grunting in the cool mud. They are quite fearsome, some of them, rearing up from their suckling pigs in a snarling threat.

"Never disturb a sow," the farmer warns. And you are reminded, with a sweet shudder, of the wild boars of fairy tale and legend.

But the little pigs, how charming, how homely, how merry! They, too, stilt impudently along on their nimble little high heels. They eye you with vacant yet saucy eyes, and flirt their pert little curly tails.

They are cowards, however. An unexpected noise, a rattling of the fence, will send them all fleeing toward the barn like a flock of frightened children. There they hover, peering cautiously out until the youngsters invite, "Sooey, sooey," when again they will come bolting and scurrying and squealing to be friends.

The Garden in the Sky

How many flowers bloom all unsuspected and unseen at the very top of the most familiar trees. How much we miss by not knowing about them, picking them, admiring them, giving them their due.

The common poplar, for instance. Our country place is full of these ordinary, taken-for-granted trees. Their trunks are an inconspicuous nun-gray; they have pleasant, four-tipped rectangular leaves. But they're "only poplars," people say; not much good for firewood—burn too fast; no good for lumber. Cut them down, make room for something else. And one of the neighbors begins an attack on his poplars, and behold! When they come crashing to the earth they bear with them a veritable mint of bloom.

The children come running with their arms full. "Look, look at all the beautiful flowers! They're like tulips, big fat tulips, on the tops of Mr. Urman's tree."

And so they are; and you have trees just like them in your own yard. To make sure, you train the field glasses on the topmost branches, and there they are—vast sky-garden, tossing their green-golden petals to the sun. The birds know and love them; they flit happily about them, chirping and singing and balancing delicately upon the strong twigs. They nest among them, these lovely cups of color unknown to most of us below.

Of a sudden the humble poplars have attained new grace and loveliness. You regard them with an astonished new respect. . . . Like people, you think. Like some people who go through life simple, modest, taken-for-granted, hiding their talents—or merely not flaunting them. Then of a sudden you discover a quality unsuspected, a wisdom, an achievement, a contribution to life quietly accomplished, a beauty undetected. "Why didn't I realize this before?" you wonder.

And then the answer comes: "I didn't raise my eyes high enough. I didn't pause to look and see."

The Sun Is a Mighty Forge

The sun holds the earth in a golden grip. People pant and fan themselves and seek the chill blessing of drinking icy water bubbling from fountains, of eating cold foods while stripped to the bare essentials.

Stores and offices assert themselves against this monster, heat, by sometimes running their air-conditioning systems so cold it shocks the senses. What was designed to be a relief, a haven, a climate wherein people can work or rest or shop in comfort, becomes in overzealous hands a place where you must wear wraps in sheer self-protection.

Yet if you can bear the heat at all, you will walk in glory. The sun is a mighty forge; it has minted a vast and dazzling fortune. Marigolds blaze in every garden, goldenrod flames in the fields. While beside each country road run the tall and glittering hordes of blackeyed Susans, wild mustard, yellow daisies. They toss their wanton petaled heads above a spume, a foam, a mist of delicate dancing grasses— nameless growths and wonders that gleam and glisten in the sun, enhanced by the lavender spikes of ironweed.

I must be descended from some tribe of tropical savages, for I am a heat lover. To me, this rampant display of later summer is even more thrilling than the finer, sweeter bursting forths of spring; the hot battering fists of August or early September are challenging. Curiously, instead of wilting before the merciless onslaught, my energies are recharged, my spirits run high.

In the heat I feel that I could almost move mountains—and take it out on furniture. This is the season when the piano must be shoved to new locations, desks hauled upstairs, beds and dressers maneuvered and cajoled and hoisted around doors into different bedrooms. All I confess, over the protests of drooping household help and dripping if strong-armed sons. To compensate, I grab the lawn mower away from them and attack the yard. Or I am inspired to do heavy cleaning, hoe the garden and build walls.

Why this strange and rather unfashionable chemistry takes place when the sun is fierce I cannot tell. Only that cold shivering doubts and denials, meek reservations and weaknesses seem literally seared out of existence. Incredibly, when the sun is tough and strong—so, like a weed, am I!

Grapes of Plenty

At dinner time your son says, "What's for dessert? Hey, y'know what'd be good? Some nice fresh grapes to eat. Or that grape cake you used to make! You know—where the grape junk went all purple and gooey through it?"

"Horrible as you make it sound, it was delicious, at that. Listen—run out to the vines on the garage, we might have some grapes in our backyard!"

"I doubt it." Your husband puts down his briefcase. "Birds got 'em nearly every year, remember? And this summer I didn't get around even to trimming them back. . . .Well, I'll be!"

He gasps as the screen door slams. For like some small triumphant god of the vineyards, his son comes trudging back, huge purple clusters in each hand. "There's millions of 'em out there, man!"

"That's funny." Your husband ponders. "But maybe not trimming the leaves was a good thing. The sun couldn't get to them, but neither could the birds!"

Whatever the reason, you all troop out and there they are, fat and ripe and ready, like rich silver-dusty pearls just waiting to be plucked. "Watch out for the bees—!" "May I take some to my new teacher tomorrow?" . . . "Make some jelly for once, will yuh, Mom?" . . . "Or grape juice, oh, boy!"

"I won't guarantee either one. But I'll make that cake you mentioned. If I can find the recipe," you add.

You return with fists and containers full. Grapes become at once appetizer, salad and dessert. The children suck them, exchange the best methods of spiting out the seeds. Argue over the dire fate of anyone who swallows them: "Grapevines might grow inside you and get all tangled up with your veins!" . . . "Aaaah. But they will give you appendicitis, won't they, Pop?"

Dishes cleared away, you begin the hunt for the long lost recipe. "If I find it we'll have the cake tomorrow," you promise. "Or bedtime if it's done."

Grape—grape—grape. You run through card files, innumerable recipe books. Grapes are such an exotic fruit, you think. Smacking of the Orient, the Italian hillside, vague pagan rites. Beautiful in paintings, or draped around other fruit in decorative bowls. But not really at home in the American kitchen, somehow. Except for the usual jam, jelly and juice, what can you do with the lovely things?

Is that why grape recipes are so rare? So actually—elusive? So that even when you've latched onto one, even then, like some will-o'-the-wisp, it disappears?

"Oh, good—here it is!" The smudged and well-worn clipping is at last in your hand. It came out before package mixes, imagine, but surely one of those on the shelf will substitute for the body of the cake itself.

The beater whirls. A winey smell comes bubbling

97

from the stove. And presently the fragrant product, "all purple and gooey," emerges from the pan. "Come and get it! Everybody that's ready for bed—"

Thick as the bees, making the same contented buzz, they swarm around, "Boy, oh, boy—are we glad you remembered. Just think—grapes in our own backyard!"

Two pounds of purple grapes—preferably from your own backyard. Three-fourths cup of sugar. Your favorite small light cake recipe, or the package kind.

Wash grapes and separate skins from pulp. Cook pulp until soft. Sieve to remove seeds. Add skins. Stir in sugar and cook until skins are tender (about 15 minutes).

There should be about two cups of pulp. Spread this over the top of your cake batter, and bake in a moderate oven about 45 minutes.

The grape layer sinks to the bottom during baking. Especially good served warm with whipped cream.

Reflections on a Lake

Some days the reflections on the lake outdo themselves. The water is more than a mirror, it is an art gallery . . . a street of busy people . . . a quiet place where lovers meet.

For all along the banks, in trees and roots and rushes are designs more intricate and yet more lovely and more free than the finest examples of modern art.

A dry jutting branch becomes a triangle in the water, a tremblingly perfect thing. Roots rear upward—and downward in duplicate, conjoining at the surface to form a shape of sheer delight. Tree trunks lean in perfect parallels; on some days they are so clear, so luminous, so complete in themselves that you could almost lift them onto a palette and hang upon a wall.

Fix the eye upon them as you pass in a boat sometime. It is like moving down the long cool vista of an art gallery where each picture rivals the last in freshness and purity and vividness of design.

Or it is like drifting down a street of fantasy and wonders. For here two dragons quarrel, with lifted paws. . . . A doctor is urging a patient, "Open wider, please, let me see your tongue." . . . A princess bends to brush her leafy hair—you see the brush, the

hand, the tresses spilling below in a bright cascade.
. . . And everywhere, everywhere willows lean to
kiss their own lips in the water, couples embrace,
countless figures in attitudes of love.

Red, Ripe Tomatoes

"Love apples," our great-grandmothers used to call tomatoes, and considered them poisonous. Dangerous, forbidden fruit. How strange it seems that the ordinary tomato should have had so exotic a reputation. Yet each year when a husband says, "Let's set out a few tomatoes—" each year when he presents, with a touch of ceremony, that first red, ripe gem, tomatoes hark back to some romantic past.

You remember the great tomato patches in the backyard gardens of childhood. The yellow stars on the ferny vines, and the vines' pungent fragrance when you brushed against them, especially at dusk. And tomatoes, sun-hot, to be eaten juicily, with salt, on a drowsy summer afternoon.

Tomatoes ripening on window sills. . . . Tomatoes bowing the branches, overflowing the bushel-baskets lugged into a kitchen where a mother was canning, and the spicy fragrance of catsup and chili sauce and piccalilli pervaded the neighborhood. . . . And the Mason jars that whispered and clicked, like people gossiping, on the back of a coal range.

And tomato juice, when people discovered it was rich in Vitamin C. And tomato soup, made lengthily from the preserved ones that marched in rosy ranks along the shelves of a cool, damp-smelling basement.

Today, for most of the year, we buy tomatoes

in stingy little packages for a price that pains. And the tomatoes are small and hard and cold, to be used sparingly, mostly to brighten a salad. Though briefly, in summer tomatoes reappear in stores or roadside stands in sufficient abundance to assume their rightful personality—fat, friendly and juicy enough to be sliced for the table, or eaten like an apple by a child.

And so when someone says, "Let's have a few tomato plants this year," it rouses up old echoes. And when he hands the first one to you grandly, it is a little like being given a slice of the days when life was simple and yet abundant, dreamy yet filled with delight. The days when succulent, edible gems enriched your own backyard.

Wings on the Wind

All about us there is a bright dipping and drifting and spilling.

Look up and see. Something is wheeling, turning delicate wings to the wind. Is it leaf or butterfly? For the butterflies are almost as numerous in their sunny flights as the leaves.

The leaves have begun to coast down. And they, too, take errant flight. A few of them skip off as if to give the butterflies gay chase. For an instant they almost collide. There is an airy dance . . . tissue-paper partners waltzing in space.

Then the leaves twirl off, begin to sink while the butterflies skim on their merry way.

Meanwhile, the birds sail blithely by, or dip down sometimes, as if curious about these gay capers. Teetering on nearby branches, they twitter accompaniment. All is light, feather-light and fragile—as ephemeral as the sunshine that sparkles everywhere.

When the Ducks Go Dancing

Evening—and the sky's gradual turning from gold to rose . . . to a deep midnight blue.

And the first bright stars appear, like early arrivals to a party. Then suddenly a flock of others join them, singly or in little sparkling clusters—so festive it seems you could hear them calling to each other if they weren't so far away.

And below, at your feet, on the glistening blue-black surface of the water the ducks are having a party too. Around the bend their first arrivals come gliding, necks undulant, weaving and circling as if testing the dance floor. Then others, singly or in little gabbling groups appear. They too call out to each other, cluster, separate, choose partners for the dance.

The orchestra is already playing. Frogs and crickets and little night things singing in rushes and grasses and trees. To all this merry music the ducks respond. In silence now, and blandly, they perform their graceful waltzes and minuets. And the patterns they draw upon the shimmering, star-spattered surface of the water are limitless, as infinite as the combinations of notes of music.

They create their white pictures, a melody of movement that must be admired, if not envied, by the fixed though sparkling stars.

A Cameo Kind of Night

It is a cameo kind of night—gently chiseled.

It is as if layer after layer has been carved away with a pure and careful knife, leaving the outlines of trees that bend above the water clean yet curiously soft. They lean in folds of loveliness over its smooth black mirror. Their edges are delicately blurred. Behind them the sky is a gray shining, almost blank of stars. Though gradually, almost diffidently the stars emerge, as if in modesty before the coming glory of the moon.

"Where is it?" your husband asks, sitting on the patio. "There's the feel of a full moon tonight—it's time for it, but where is it?"

"It's coming," you inform him confidently. "It's slow but it'll be here—see how much brighter a glow there is behind us to the left."

As you speak its force intensifies; it pours through the spaces of the nearest branches—you see its fiery rim and then the full majesty of its face. It is like a great prince mounting the sky in a slow and stately tread. How can it hurry, this thing so full of splendor? It is weighted, it is restrained by its own burden, its own vast bowl of fiery light.

And the evening itself is respectful, like the stars. There is no shouting, no noise of wind and wave. Even the children, bent over their homework up in the cabin, are curiously quiet. No dogs bark, no frogs thump and call. Except for the steady little stringed orchestra of crickets, the moon's coming is met by silence. This—all this—is muted, cameo bright and small and soft.

It is a cameo kind of night.

Fall

Birdsong and Cider-Sweet Air

Do the birds sing a sweeter song in the fall? Or does it only seem so because the air itself is so clear and brightly shining that it too almost sings?

The sunlight rioting through the golden mesh of the trees . . . the leaves wheeling down. Do the birds try to match this color and brilliance by chiming and trilling and sending forth their own gaudy ribbons of sound?

Or are they perhaps like people about to depart on a journey, exchanging reminiscences, and crying out their lilting, exuberant farewells.

Do they discuss the nests long empty and abandoned, the little ones flown off to feed and chirp and test the new wonder of their wings?

Do the parent birds congratulate each other and exult at the summer's achievement? Do they warn each other of perils to come on the journey ahead?

Whatever it is—whatever—the birds have tuned up all the shining instruments at their command. And the paean of their singing is an added shower of loveliness on autumn air that is cider-sweet.

The Strange Perfume of Fall

What is this strange perfume of fall?

It is faintly spicy, sharp and tingling, and very old.

In the morning it assails the senses with its bright tang, lively and fresh as perking coffee.

In the afternoon it is warm and deep, still stirring, but almost serene. But it is best in the evening when the dew has fallen. Then it seems to wake, to throb; its fragrance is exotic.

Walking across the damp rustling yard on a moonlit night, you find the fragrance is a real thing, a kind of insistent presence invading the blood. It is as old as the Pyramids; it speaks of long-ago people in distant places—ancestors camping on ancient hillsides.

Or it speaks to us of forests when our own country was new and mysterious. Of fires in little log huts, with Indians lurking nearby—thrilling, vaguely threatening and strange.

Yet its message is immediate too. Now . . . now; It seems to be whispering as you scuff through the fallen leaves. Breathe it. Taste it, feel it. Drink deeply of the wine of today.

A Back

What a beautiful thing is a back!

Yes, a plain old-fashioned human back. Especially a back held straight and firm. Like my mother before me, I hate to see people slouch, especially at the table. I am forever urging offspring, "Sit up straight, throw your shoulders back."

For a back is a barometer of emotions and self-esteem. A straight back announces "gumption" (another old-fashioned word), courage, pride, determination. It seems to me that people who bend over unduly are saying something sad about themselves. Signaling to the world that they feel unworthy, or that life has been treating them badly, or that maybe they want to become small and crouching and go creeping away into some hiding place.

The military has always had the right psychology in making men and women march with rigidly straight backs. Heads up, chins square, shoulders back. (Let's hope they don't scrap that too, along with KP and spit-shined shoes in their foolish campaign to make the services more alluring.) I love the beauty of marching men for this reason, the sheer command of muscles. And of dancers and models too, trained to discipline the supple muscles of their lovely backs. And of Polynesian or Arab women carrying jugs or bundles on their heads or shoulders with that superb and graceful balance that comes from a straight back.

It is my fervent conviction that self-discipline through life, a continual awareness of the value of good posture, can prevent not only much back trouble but bent backs. Yet not all people have been taught this, and many people have been forced to carry many burdens.

So a bowed back can be beautiful, too. The back that has been curved and thickened by age, infirmity or labors. "I have lived much, endured much, carried much," it says with a quiet eloquence. So whenever I see one I am touched—that a support once strong and straight should have been pulled down, like a fine tree weighted by its fruit.

In any case, it's a beautiful thing to see and to have—that marvel, a human back.

Morning Light

How beautiful is morning light across a country lake. "Get up, get up!" it urges, stealing into the room. How silent its golden invasion, yet how insistent. It seems to draw you, half-protesting, from the snug nest of bed.

You follow its path across an old pine floor. The kitchen is still dusky, yet a pale patina falls across the surfaces of things. Counter and kettles are touched with a fragile brush, promising warmth. Shivering, you turn on burners and in their glow don your bathing suit.

Recent floods have left the rock steps muddy. They are soft and cracked to your bare feet, descending. Across the water, the low growths of brush and branches are gray from its recent rushing assault. Now the water lies bland, subdued, gray-green, painted with the growing light, which turns all this muddy ochre to a broad and pleasing stripe. The light heightens the gray roof of a rust-red cabin and its stone walls. It lifts the whole cabin and places it in duplicate upon the morning mirror of the lake.

The light, with its warmth, has not penetrated the water. The dark depths are fiercely cold. Even the surface, when you rise, still clings to the chilled-wine cold. No—such warmth as you find must be your own. You strike out toward some rocks that, like the kitchen, wear a mantle of pale new light. Yet they glitter too when you cling to them, darken them with dripping water. The sky is a soft, bland blue. A thin ghost scrap of moon gazes down.

The light is stronger when you climb out. Strong enough for shadows. There is the sparkle and the shadow of changing leaves. The shadow of the over-turned canoe. A boat churning by carries its clear bright twin below. A couple who fish early every day call out, their lifted hands like little salutes to morning.

In the kitchen the kettle chuffs and blows its merry whistle. The coffee, when you have dressed in slacks and sweater, matches the warmth inside. Birds are singing, and so is your blood, your whole being. The whole world is awake and shining now, joining forces with the warmth and the joy of morning light.

I think sometimes that I'd like to be a crow. Yes, a stupid, noisy, yelling, commonplace crow.

Oh, it would be lovely to be a heron, soaring on mysterious and elegant wings.

Or, perhaps a little bird—a hummingbird, hovering like a fairy's helicopter above a flower. Or any of the whole golden school of tiny birds—canaries, orioles, yellow warblers, light-hearted and singing as they dart about, as if always going to parties.

Or there's something enviably appealing about a woodpecker, saucy and bright-throated, tapping so furiously upon a tree as if to say, "Now I know you're in there—open the door!"

I wouldn't care much to be a sparrow, or even a robin, despite the spurt of excitement a first robin causes in the spring. These birds are such humdrum little beings, rather plain and well—middle-class.

No, if I couldn't be a really colorful or dramatic bird, I'd rather be a big black low-class crow.

Each morning, a flock of them wakes us with their raucous commotion. Caw, caaw, CAAW! they shout, voices grating and jangling like rusty keys.

They sound like a bunch of beer bums, far gone in riotous living. Yaaa, yaaa, yaaa! they jeer at the world and each other. Okay, so you're another! Caaaw, caaaw, caaaw!

What a beautiful battle of sound and feathers. The trees rock and shake with it, though the leaves keep trying to shush them.

"Shhh, tone it down, you're waking everybody up." But the crowd couldn't care less. "Mind your own business," cry these bawdy baritones. "We've been thrown out of better joints than this." And off they go, wings flapping in a drunken grace across the streets of the sky.

Oh, the freedom! The sheer, intoxicating delight. To never have to worry about what to wear—only be garbed like these hags of heaven in safe shiny black. To be able to yell without considering the neighbors. To tell everybody off, family, friends, the world. And then after a glorious fight just to go winging away—flap-flap-flap.

Lean Closer to the Stars

A window is a square hole cut or left in a house. A rectangular block suddenly open and unconfining when you fling up the glass. A frame that is lovely for leaning.

Lean out of an upstairs window some night. Lean out and look out to find peace, release and freedom. You are close to infinity there in a top floor window, and close to yourself.

The sky seems vast, far yet near, an expanse in which you can almost be lifted, soar, go gaily and bodilessly gliding. The stars are aloof in their shining, but they appear near too, near enough to touch. They are hung there like lamps for your pleasure, lamps that you may reach out and brighten or dim.

Clouds swing across the face of a moon that grins as if urging, "Come join me." The air tastes cool and sweet up here. It is soft yet tingling, fragrant with spring.

In the distance cars move, incessant glowworms burrowing through the night. But here all is still except for the voice of the hurrying creek. It never rests, it babbles and discusses without ceasing—yet now and then there is a difference in its tones, as when people pause for breath. You think of the church socials of childhood, or cocktail parties, the meaningless jumble of voices. The creek glides by like the clouds, on light liquid feet, effortless and quick.

The water winks and explodes with small diamonds of moonlight, the rocks wear gems. Suddenly the words of a half-forgotten song begin to sing in tune to the creek's liquid music: "The best things in life are free!" They really are. This square of space. This backyard kingdom; these jeweled rocks, those bright gemmed lamps overhead. Night IS free, and you couldn't buy a star if you tried.

They are yours just for being alive. When you can perch in an upstairs window who needs to be rich?

Instead You Want to Sing

You run into the backyard with the dog on a busy morning, irked because the beast has been barking, and fuming because nobody's taken her out before.

And snapping the leash to the chain on the clothesline that will give her running room, you wheel to find a spray of scarlet dogwood leaves flaming and dancing at you, like fire on a grate.

And a neighbor calls a cheery, "Good Morning!" around the pins in her mouth as she fastens dazzling white sheets to her own clothesline. Then the milkman waves from his big, equally white truck sailing by. And you hear the birds running little scales and trills and calling to the world and to each other from the sun-filled trees.

And you realize suddenly that the morning is so breathless, so bursting with good humor and delight that instead of scolding you want to sing!

Oh, What a Beautiful War

The trees, like merry knights, wear mail of gold and silver that flashes in the sunlight. Their helmets are plumed in scarlet, they fly banners of purple and bronze.

While night and day we hear their brisk bombardments. The acorn bullets rattle and snap on cars and streets and roofs—and heads.

The squirrels, like fervent little scouts, scurry in and out of the battle lines, going about the mysterious business of retrieving or burying.

Blackbirds join the excitement. They swoop down, in formation, glittering and screeching, to occupy the vivid golden territory of the trees. They advance across the bright-strewn lawn, they breech the garden wall.

"Look, look!" a son summons you one night from getting dinner—and you rush to witness the battle. The bold and lively war that is being waged in your own backyard: Lithe brown bodies are leaping and bounding, black ones zooming. What a clashing and crying, what a fury of cascading shot and shell of acorns and twigs, with even the leaves involved. They shimmer, they advance, retreat and in a golden shower come clamoring down.

If ever a beautiful war could be waged it is this one, witnessed each year in your own backyard!

Laborers in the Yard

Barebacked workmen and strong young sons at their labors in the yard.

Their muscles are almost the same red-clay color as the soil they are shoveling, or the bronze of the turning leaves.

The bowing trees above them, and the curved road beyond the rock wall they are building. . . . The road is gray-blue and so are their faded jeans.

The faithful old cement mixer churning, its voice a throaty background for their voices, and the sounds of morning—birds singing and an occasional car going by.

The obliques and curves of the scene—a continually shifting pattern of bent backs, shoveling arms, a pair of legs striding up a slope behind a wheelbarrow. . . . The mounds of moist red earth, the piles of white rocks, the cones of dark gravel and golden sand.

The sun laces and stripes all this with its own mobile patterns as the wind stirs the bending trees. It is a picture of movement—peaceful, constructive, beautiful. As beautiful now, in this moment, as it will be when the wall is finished. Perhaps more so. For then these homely tools and materials and muscles will have vanished from the scene.

The Muted Shining

It is a misty, moisty night as you set off, reluctantly, to walk the dog. But the moon is a blurred white flower struggling to bloom, and the air is crisp yet warm.

The white dog joyfully tugs you down the black shining hill. And the youngest cat has slipped out and pats silently behind, white face and paws echoing the Dalmation's spotted body in tinier dots that weave through the dark, dripping shadows. They are like little floating stars or petals in the half-shiny dark.

There is a strange muted shining all about. The trees are touched with silver, the piles of wet leaves shimmer faintly in the ditch. Yard lamps burn yellow on their posts, like rigid tulip flames. And little pools on grass and pavement mirror both shadows and the soft, muted light.

A low-flying plane moves leisurely overhead, wing lights winking, throat throbbing as if in song. In the distance a siren begins to bawl like a beast in torment. Soon come the flashing red lights, great engine swooping around the corner, men in shiny black coats clinging. But even this is cheerful, adding action and adventure to the lazily ticking night.

The dog barks madly, longing to pursue. A frisky young German shepherd trots genially up, and both dogs sniff, pant and issue threatening growls. Then the stranger turns frantic attention to the cat, sending her streaking up a tree. She quivers there, indignant little white face spitting, comical goblin of the night.

You rescue her, and holding her softness to your cheek, run on home behind the dog.

The Ladder

A ladder lying among the unraked leaves. . . .

It sprawls there like a hoyden, long and naked and lean. It is partly covered by the equally indolent accusation of the leftover, tawny wet leaves. It thrusts its feet impudently out of their careless covering.

"Why didn't somebody put me away?" it seems to grin, friendly and casual. Not really caring—just sprawling there in a kind of simple abandon where it was flung down last fall. As if it had really enjoyed the long winter's slumber under the leaves. (And you can understand this—wouldn't it be lovely to fling yourself down and just go to sleep for weeks cuddled in the crisp abundance of the leaves?) But now the wind has come poking and stirring, revealing the slug-a-bed. The skinny body, the sturdy rungs, the out-thrust feet.

Somebody must be summoned to go out and put it away. (Before tackling those leaves!) One of the boys, who must have left it there in the first place. And tracking down the culprit, issuing instructions, you remember the day he had propped the ladder against a tree to rescue a plaintively mewing kitty—the oblique line of it, the shadow of its rungs, and your own whimpering plea to be careful, not to fall and break his neck. . . . But the ladder held fast, boy and cat came safely down, to your immense relief. And the memory comes back with a sense of joy and tenderness, as you see the ladder lying among the leaves.

A Walk in the Rain

It is dusk, and a light rain falling, when your daughter calls from her dancing studio. She'll be leaving in a few minutes, can you meet her bus? Your husband is out of town; no car is available, but it will be pleasant to walk.

Your son rushes to get the raincoat of which he is so proud. It reaches almost to his heels; he peers out of its helmet like a miniature knight in armor. You reach for your daughter's rain gear, tie a scarf on and set off into the wet cool evening.

The rain comes down gently, with a steady but unhurried pace, ticking rhythmically on the silken umbrella, bouncing like silver arrows from the street. The gutters run frothily, and on top of the gushing current ride big round bubbles that, for some reason, your youngster has always called frogs. He endows them with voices now—"Chug-a-rum, chug-a-rum!"

From lighted windows you are aware of people settling down with their coffee, their evening papers and programs. Their broad yards are green and bright with flowers. Chrysanthemums are clutches of color on fences—yellow, pink, blood red, and the petals that the rain has earlier beaten off lie like scattered confetti.

You walk up a hill, where a concrete bridge spans the creek. Its rows of arch-necked lights cast yellow ribbons across the wet sidewalk. The traffic of early evening roars by—buses, trucks, the late worker homeward bound. Beyond, blurring another hill, are the merging, blending greens and golds of trees, and behind them the soft steel-gray of the evening sky.

In the wooden shelter the rain pecks at the roof with its tiny beaks. The knight mounts the bench and marches back and forth, still calling to the "frogs." It is cozy and somehow secret, waiting for the bus. Soon you see its great yellow eyes swinging round the bend. It halts and your daughter descends, carrying her dancing bag. She is lithe and lovely, with her hair soft about her shoulders. She puts on the red plaid coat you have brought, belts it tight about her waist. She takes the umbrella now, and holds its silken glove over you as you set off, pressed close, chatting about her lesson.

The young knight lags behind, sloshing through puddles. It is a moment before you realize that he has crossed the street. There he marches comically along, with a kind of sober determination that makes you laugh. At the corner, however, he halts in obvious distress, where the water runs deep.

You go to his rescue, wetting your feet, and carry him safely to a dry island. There he struggles down and rushes on ahead, toward the lights of home which pour their banners across the shining grass. Your daughter, eager with hunger, darts after him with her swift dancer's step. For an instant, in the lights and the mist, with her skirts and her bright hair flowing, she recreates the ballet.

You linger, reluctant to leave the gentle ticking loveliness. You gaze down on the rushing, gabbling water of the creek. You admire the rock garden glittering on a neighbor's bank. Then you, too, enter the warm, quiet, food-scented house.

The Bright Receiving Line

Driving along the parkways, especially toward evening, is like going down a shining receiving line of trees.

They beam at you with their sunlit faces, they bow and stretch out their gilded arms. They are all attired in party dress, vying in their splendor of bronze and gold and scarlet and plum and tangerine.

They are dignified, however. They stand with the composure of titled personages accustomed to being admired. They do not thrust themselves upon you. They are simply there, gracious and serene.

"How gorgeous you are," you long to blurt as each seems to outdo the other. "What a glorious party, what a beautiful fall."

"How nice of you to say so," they seem to be replying. "We're so glad you enjoy it, so happy you are here."

The Deer

What a thrill it is to visit a place where deer are almost as common as falling leaves. And almost the selfsame color as many leaves' dusty autumn hues, for nature has cleverly designed their disguise. The eye must hunt them as you drive along these western roads. And they are more likely to be seen at evening when they rouse from whatever slumberous dreams deer have by day, and emerge to eat.

The car slows down or stops, and there across the weathered rail fences a proud antlered buck will return your breathless gaze. Still . . . so still. Frozen in this attitude, thinking himself unseen. Then, at the slightest disturbance, off he sails, light as down, nimble and weightless as men who travel to the moon.

Most common are the does and their fawns. Among the brush you spy them, their bodies the same delicate pale gray-brown shade as the dry fallen trunks and branches. Nature has painted them with a loving brush, softly, gently, to match their surroundings, then whimsically finished off her handwork with a jaunty white flag of tail.

The Warmth of Friends and Fireplace

The wind is in competition with the sun. It catches the light-gilded leaves and sends them scudding. A bird, out to coast in the bright morning sky, is swept into orbit and gets a free ride. The water, silver-paved, runs frantically before it, the waves like a flock of children chasing each other. The boats rock and lunge.

While inside your country cabin, the fire on the grate is disturbed. It begins to send out a protesting blue film of smoke.

Then suddenly the lights go off, the TV fades in the middle of a program, the little kitchen radio stops in the middle of a song. "Daddy, something's the matter," the children say. "Nothing'll work—" and he makes for the fuse box.

Before he gets there, there is a rapping on the door and a neighbor in a plaid jacket as bright as the leaves, asks, "You folks got any electricity down here?"

"No, we thought it was just a fuse," you tell him. "Come in."

In a minute another windblown neighbor has arrived with the same question. "Must be a branch blown down on a line." You all agree, and phone the power company, which tells you yes, yes, they know and are already working on it, though it may take quite a while.

"Sit down, sit down," you tell everybody, for emergencies seem to create a party mood. "Let's have some coffee."

You go to the stove to heat it up, get down the thick old-fashioned mugs that seem to make country coffee taste better, especially at times like this. But when you start to pour it you stop short, feeling foolish. "It's cold!"

"Of course, stupid," everybody laughs. "How did you expect to heat it on a cold electric stove?"

"But we've just got to have coffee. I know what —the fireplace!"

You set the pot tipsily against the coals and in a few minutes it begins to steam and sing. You reach in to get it and jump back, for the handle is scorching hot. With the aid of a bright checked towel, you pour it, pass it around. Another log is added to the fire, which begins to boast, "Who needs electricity with me on the job?" But the wind retorts with another gust, which causes it to smoke and choke.

Your husband opens the door a little to let the smoke escape. The sunshine, seeing its chance, floods the room. But the wind comes romping on its heels, and both must be shut firmly out once more. You sit talking about fireplaces and the part they played in the days before Ben Franklin helped to harness the usually dependable servant, electricity.

The wind laughs at the lot of you huddled so helplessly around the hearth. But the coffee is hot and delicious and the time of sharing it one of those unexpected pleasures that make life so good.

A Doorknob

Pause sometime to admire a doorknob. A simple, everyday doorknob of brass or copper, or old-fashioned wood. Sometimes handsomely carved, or merely sculptured and smoothed by the fingers that turn it and touch it each day.

How blindly we do this. How unconsciously we reach out toward that circle of substance that gives us entrance to a house or a room. Who ever really LOOKS at a doorknob, except a housewife bent on scrubbing or shining it? Or her husband repairing it when, incredibly, it falls off or refuses to budge?

Or—Oh, yes, when you're building a house. Then the vast variety of doorknobs is suddenly visible to you in full array. You examine them with true awareness, you pick and choose. But soon, all too soon, doorknobs vanish from our consciousness, are absorbed into the blind routine of living.

Yet doorknobs deserve a bit of loving respect. What would we do without them? Even inanimate objects are swimming with life, scientists tell us. Or at least an atomic activity that is closely akin to it. And while I don't claim that doorknobs have minds to really see and appreciate all the little, lovely things surely they must vibrate with the hands that have a mute vitality. And to be a full person, living one's own life to the utmost, we should sometimes stop to really see and appreciate all the little, lovely things that play a part in our day.

The Merry Battle

October is a month of merry battle between wind and sun.

They vie for possession of the water. They snatch at it and toss it about and divide it up between them into shining black areas and patches and V's of twinkling radiance. While the trees that bend above it cast down their bright secret votes for one or the other.

There is a steady rustling sound, a rhythmic ticking as the leaves descend, to ride the black and silver surface softly, lightly, now like an armada of ships assembling to join the fray.

And the wind and the sun quarrel between them over people as well. Leaving to go fishing, you too are subject to this lovely spirited tug-of-war. The air is brisk; in deference to the breeze you wear slacks and a flannel shirt, and bind back your hair. But before you reach the boat you feel the sun's warm seductive assault. "Wait, I think I'll change to shorts," you decide; but just to be safe you carry along warmer gear as well.

The hour or two you spend at the fallen tree where the bass lurk is a constant on-again, off-again performance with your clothes. The sun's embrace is so warm you can feel it through shirt and sweater.

But no sooner have you yielded than the wind swoops down.

Meanwhile, the leaves continue to fall, twisting, rustling, talking it over, undecided, but favoring both sides with their radiance.

Preview of Paradise

Sometimes the sea is almost too beautiful to behold. Almost too much of loveliness has been poured upon its shining breast.

The sky has emptied itself of its treasures; the very gates of heaven have been melted to send their gold cascading down. The sea is paved with its effulgence. It is a vast gemmed street traced with paths of purest silver where peacocks strut, fiery-feathered.

It is almost too dazzling for the eyes to follow or the soul to comprehend. One wonders at such moments: Is all this perhaps a preview? Are we given such glimpses here in preparation for Paradise?

Ironing Board Bonuses

The pleasure of fitting a new cover to your ironing board. Pulling and tugging and pinning and patting until it's smooth and white as a snowy hillside. . . .

The perfumed haze of spray starch, a kind of gay airy kiss that makes the clothes supple and ready to cooperate with the iron. . . .

Your iron beginning to purr and chuff as if in anticipation. As eager and faintly comical as The Little Engine that kept saying, "I think I can, I think I can!" (And surveying the basket piled high, you think the engine may be speaking for you.) . . .

The crumpled, defeated look of a boy's shirt before you take it in hand. Like a troubled son who comes to you for guidance, and begins to buck up, take shape, smile and finally to brag. . . .

The good crisp snap of a pillow slip as you shake it into readiness. The subtle comfort of the flatwork, swift and easy and as effortless as talking with uncritical friends. . . .

The patterns that you'd never otherwise really see for what they are: The flowers and birds and intricate entwinings, the checks and stripes and dots, the many blendings of color—in an apron, a paisley skirt, a blouse, a pair of curtains or a tablecloth.

These are some of the nicest bonuses of this job that so many of us dread and put off. The ironing board becomes an unwitting showcase for bits of beauty we'd never otherwise observe.

Trees Stand Pure Against the Sky

Look out the kitchen windows as you cook. The trees are tall friends standing by. Like people, alike in so many respects, yet each so enthrallingly different. Their trunks are the soft color of pewter or ashes. Some are mottled and splotched, as if they've been the target of a child's paint pot. Here and there the slender birches are stripes of chalky white.

How their trunks soar upward, strong and joyous with the freedom of boughs uncluttered by leaves. They are like tall-bodied women unclothed the better to dance or merely to stretch into the cold tingling embrace of wind and sky.

Only the oaks still wear their leafy sweaters. Their early brilliance long since faded, now they are sleeved and scarved in stubborn wrappings the color of Indian moccasins, worn and soft and old.

How the branches of trees reach out to admire themselves. How they curve and lift and turn, jut upwards, droop low, each in a sculpture unique unto itself. Look down any avenue of trees, no matter how similar, and you will find no two the same.

Fall is the season when trees seem to be saying, with that eloquent silence only trees can assume: "Look, oh look at me!"

Trees stand pure against the sky these days. Only the frail penned pattern of twigs gets between——and it in a delicate, wispy fashion, as a veil enhances the charm of a woman's face.

The pines climb the hill in battalions, stand patiently at attention before the spectacle of the sky. Their crowns make a lacey fretwork against its lemon-yellow that slowly begins to flame and burn, as if to consume their delicate intricacies. Then swiftly the sunset retreats. The fires bow, sink to a few glowing embers that are held briefly in the patient, tender fingers of the trees.

And suddenly, almost before you have turned from setting the table, this too has vanished, become a lavender-gray nothingness behind the black eternal meshings of the boughs.

The Inviting Adventure of Steps

How clever is man that he invented steps. Those sturdy boxes for human feet—how useful, and how beautiful. Any kind of steps. Not merely those that lead up long, lovely flights of stairs; not only richly carpeted steps, however we enjoy them, or even brilliantly polished steps. Just—steps.

Look sometime at a flight of steps. There is a native artistry about them—their lovely parallels. And the very word "flight" connotes lightness—the feet that fly up them or scurry down. Though steps must be sound and strong. (And all the feet that climb them do not fly; no, some feet negotiate steps slowly.)

Steps are inviting. It's fun to explore or to live in a house with unexpected steps. To step up or down into a room—how intriguing. Impossible to take it for granted, you have moved onto a different plane and so are more AWARE of where you are. And steps are fun to follow, little surprises that lead down into a garden or up a pathway to a hill.

Curved steps are especially fascinating. The body must curve in response. Not rectangles now, they are pie-shaped wedges, but all neatly echoing each other. . . . The Scots have many curved stone steps in their buildings in Scotland. They splay gracefully before you like a furl of pleated ruffles or an opened fan.

And steps are significant. How many public monuments must first be reached by ascending a long flight of steps. As the body makes its effort to get there the spirit is being prepared as well; our expectation rises for the moment of awe when we arrive. Artists and architects know this; it is one reason why so many monuments are placed on elevations, silhouetted against the sky.

As many people get older they cannot manage so many steps. And there are others who dread steps, find them a handicap. What a pity. To miss the sheer pleasure of climbing steps. Run up and down steps if you can. I love to. It's wonderful exercise. And if you can make it a habit when you're young, you're likely to keep nimble and be able to enjoy steps all your life.

Street Lamps Beside the River

The river lies black and shining, coins of brightness blazing on its satin breast. The wind strikes at
them, breaks and shatters them into little snakes and
scribbles of gold, silver, scarlet, flame. Then they
fall into place once more, coins and sequins and
scattered gems. . . .

On the far banks the street lamps form rhythmic
looping patterns of light and shadow. Each light
burns at the crest, like a lovely star hung in a steeple.
The lights shine mystically and serenely, staving off
the darkness, offering little tented shelters of brightness in the night.

Get Up, Get Up!

How sad it seems not to be able to sleep when you have the chance. When the house is quiet, when nobody's sick to call you and nobody's missing to worry about. And yet, to have the mind resist this lovely circumstance with its incessant chatter and probings and plannings. And despite every formula you've ever learned, you just can't make it shut up.

And then, to your dismay, light comes—it's morning! Though a frantic look at the clock reveals it's at least a couple of hours before it's really time to get up. . . . And yet why not, since it's more wretched not to? Instead of lying here, fighting the futile battle, why not escape it, maybe gain a few laps in the day's coming race?

And so you crawl out, rather crossly—and the rewards begin to spill all over you. Sunrise! How long since you've seen it? But there it is blasting across the sky in unbelievable splendor. And a cup of coffee all by yourself, with a book to read uninterrupted—what rare delight! The burner is as rosy as the sunrise, heating up the pot. The mug in your hand is cozy.

A big chair by the window—and behold, birds breakfasting at the feeder, chattering and quarreling. The pink light enhances their colors, and how vividly green are the trees.

The dog, roused from her own deep slumbers, yawns and comes padding to nuzzle your knee. The cat leaps onto your lap. Stroking them, you look about and find the house so silent, strangely lovely even in its clutter—the lamps, the plants, the paintings on the wall. Peace and pride touch you in a curious new way, a sense of some dearness unremarked before.

Is that perhaps why the mind clamored so insistently these past hours? Was some more essential voice trying to tell you, "Get up, get up?"

This Bright Waiting

Most of the trees stand still and waiting, reaching out their empty arms as if feeling for the flutter of flakes to come. Meanwhile, leaves whip about unraked yards, reckless as children on a holiday, calling, "Catch me if you can!"

They are bangled and bright with sun. The sun sparkles on the evergreen laurel that so staunchly claims summer, whatever the season. It pokes and strokes its brightness about the oaks who stubbornly cling to their final copper clothing. How patient these oaks. How superior to mere fashions that signal a season. They are like well-dressed women who select only the best and wear it with some instinctive, superior knowledge, and discard it only when it pleases them. One never knows whether they are ahead or behind of the season; one is only suitably impressed.

All this the snow will settle when it's ready. When it, too, decides the time has come. It will powder the tall, searching trees, fur them snugly. Even the oaks will be altered, and the deep insistent laurel's green. The scampering leaves on the lawn will be stilled at last, tucked soundly into their deep white beds. "Hush," the snow will whisper, "settle down."

But meanwhile—ah, but meanwhile there is this bright waiting. The lovely ungilded time of in-between!

November Urges "Hurry Home!"

November is a steely month. The sky is the color of a new-forged blade, and its bite is sometimes as sharp. Nature, so bountiful a mother a little while back, is now the ruthless surgeon, scalpel in hand, paring, stripping clean.

The trees are mostly barren. They make a lonely creaking in the night, as if mourning for the leaves so recently held in their arms. And the leaves, like little lost children, run frantically across the frosted grasses, or tap with tightly curled fists at windows and doors.

There is a cozy feeling about November, a sense of the joy of coming inside for keeps after the long late autumn, of contented settling down. November is the kind of month that urges, "Hurry home!"

Winter

Sunrise Is the Reason

Some mornings you wake early for no good reason, and are nudged out of bed for no good reason, except—"Well, I'm not going to sleep any more, so I might as well start the day."

And you pull the shades for no good reason and glance outside for no good reason except to measure the kind and weather of this day.

But your eyes are drawn upward for a very good reason, and you gasp for a very good reason: The sky is telling you to feast your eyes fast. Because right now the sun is a glorious gold, thrusting long fingers out . . . out . . . as if to clasp and claim and decorate the turbulent canvas of the clouds.

Gray clouds, layers and banks of gray clouds stretching across the sky; coral at the centers, purple at the peaks, but mostly that soft secretive gray that means they could be stirring up a batch of trouble. But meanwhile witness this lovely display of finger painting. This strong bright stroking and shading before its darker intentions can be revealed.

And now you realize the reason—the very good reason—something prodded you out of bed.

Nature Indoors

How much of nature we bring indoors to love and enjoy on cold winter days. How much of its taste, its colors, its warmth. Instinctively we do this, I think. Like squirrels hoarding their acorns, we too are creatures driven to capture the comforts of summer and fall against the days when our doors must be closed.

Build a big fire and hear it crackling and chuckling on the grate. Watch its flames embrace the logs. Once the wood that feeds it was a tall old maple tree in the yard. It held a child's rope swing and nested the birds that came to the feeder—bluebirds and cardinals and juncos and jays. How green were its leaves in summer, and how brilliant their gold when October came.

Then a night of storm and lightning brought it crashing down. And you cut it up and stacked it and kept it for this hour. And in the flames that leap and play about it now you see again its colors—the green and scarlet and gold of its leaves, and the lovely birds flashing about in their coats of blue and red and gray. See too the children's hair flying as they swang, the flipping of bright little skirts and scarves. Listen . . . you can even hear the voices of birds and children laughing and chirping from the fire. And its memories warm you even as it cheers and warms your house.

On the mantel above the fire is a brass jug of dried flowers. Strawflowers and baby's breath and goldenrod and honesty that you planted and tended. Once tossing bright in the garden, filled with their living juices, they caught and cupped the sun. And now brittle and still, they continue to claim the summer's colors.

And the kitchen—ah, the kitchen, the pantry, the freezer. Just as our mothers and grandmothers stocked their caves and cellars, we too stock nature's bounty (and its memories) against the cold:

Blackberry jam in a jar. . . . It brings back the days when you and the children braved the brambles to fill your buckets with those dark beauties big as your thumbs.

The ranks of canned tomatoes on a shelf. . . . Their rosy cheeks peering through the glass are once again the scarlet globes you wrested from the ferny fragrance of the vines.

The purple grape juice in its bottles, the amber of cider and sweet wine. . . . Pour a glass of any of these, lift it to the light; sniff its special aroma, taste it, savor it with all your senses. These juices too are nature's ways of warming our blood indoors.

Even the cold breath of the freezer holds nature in wintry bounty: The bright green packets of peas and beans, the yellows of string beans and limas and corn, the reds of raspberries and strawberries and cherries. . . .

To choose from this generous storehouse is to restore summer to our table. To bring back again the beauty and wonder of nature long after we've closed our doors.

Boxes

What a marvelous thing is a box!

Even the name "box" has a pert smack to it. So brief to hold so much promise . . . so much utility, yes, so much homely everyday service—yet so much excitement too, especially with Christmas approaching. So much suspense.

"What's in the box?" From earliest childhood we are eager to know. Those big brown boxes that the postman delivers, excitingly, to the door. Those enticingly wrapped boxes of all sizes and shapes for birthdays or holidays. The mystery they contain! All held within that rectangle that is itself so satisfying to the hands and eye.

Learning to draw a box is a child's first exercise in geometry: Pencil, paper—a clumsily fashioned square. Then another line to the right and a little below; then adjoining lines—and lo, he has made a box. A transparent box. And by erasing some lines he can make the box solid and secret, a box nobody can see into; a box he can fill with any toys and treasurers he imagines. By drawing a few more lines he can even tie it up with ribbons and a bow.

And so the thrill of the box begins . . . and most of us never outgrow it. A box becomes something special.

Most of life's gifts come in boxes; and so many

of life's delights: New shoes and crayolas and paint sets and party dresses and wedding dresses and china and silver and baby clothes.

And the sturdy stuff of everyday living comes mostly in boxes: Cereal. Eggs. Apples in rough wooded boxes whose fragrances mingle with that of the fruit they hold. . . . Bakery cakes sheltered in fragile cardboard boxes. . . . Boxes of books, boxes of papers, boxes of clothes.

Almost no day passes that we don't turn to a box for help. To carry things, to pack things in when we move. To send things in—presents to people, clothes and cookies to children away from home. And to store things in. We pack up our lives in boxes: Souvenirs of trips taken, keepsakes, diaries, old letters.

What dear dependable friends boxes are. So much so that we are reluctant to throw them out. There is something almost disloyal about it. Something that warns, "Don't." (For who knows when you might need them?) And so our piles of boxes accumulate—even though, contrarily, it's always hard to find the right size when you want one.

Even so, a box is reassurance. A box is a humble, rectangular framework and summary of the needs and joys of life.

The lake is solid now. It wears a steely sheath. It is a vast flat vault in which the water is locked away. At night you hear the muffled moaning of the water, as if striving against its fate. By day it makes a more cheerful noise, a kind of merry cracking. Far and high above it a V of geese go honking . . . faint, faint their thrilling cries replying. (Oh, to join them —to go flying off, wherever they go, with the geese!)

The ducks come picking their way around the rocks and rusty banks where only the crowfoots and holly and firs remind you of summer's green. Quacking and quarreling they come, a waddling white-clad inspection committee, to gingerly test the edges of this, their former realm. One ventures forth, another follows, slipping comically, making little skidding circles while the others observe. The leader lifts, skims back to shore, and off they all march single file, indignantly scolding.

The skaters have already done their exploring. Each day more and bolder ones come swooping. Impossible to restrain the family any longer; they've had their skates ready for weeks. Down the banks they too scurry like a caged flock released. Soon they also are wobbling about like the ducks, then skimming free.

You watch from the window, torn between concern, pride, envy and something like dread. All you really want to do is curl up content by the fire with a good book. Yet those voices below . . . calling, calling . . . calling to something within you, like the geese. Resigned to it now you dig out your own pair, a daughter's scuffed and grubby hand-me-downs. Bundled up against the bitter cold, and with a last longing look at the tempting fire, you slam the door.

Their shouts of welcome warm you. And as you perch on a rock to shove a foot into that cozy yet familiar nest of shoe, a son crouches to help you. It makes you think of long ago days when brothers and neighbor boys performed this gallantry for girls. (Please let's not yield that to Women's Lib!) One of the laces snaps as he pulls it tight.

"Mom, *when* are you going to get a decent pair of skates?"

"I don't skate that much," you grin when he's knotted it and pulls you to your feet

You cling to his sturdy arm as ankles curl. There is always this moment when you're sure you can't do it, you'll fall, break something, disgrace yourself. . . . Then you let go and are staggering off on your own, getting reacquainted with the slippery tricks of ice and blade. Soon miraculously you too are gliding, circling, drawing your own silver whorls among the patterns on the glossy pavement. Your feet are contributing to the sweet hissing music of the other skates. You can do it, you can do it! So swerve out and away.

You salute the bare trees onshore seen in some radiant new perspective from this windswept expanse. The houses and cabins with their smoke wreathing up—how different they look from here, so vividly blue and white and green against the gray. Like a paper doll village set down amongst the black branchings of the trees—look out, they will blow away.

You too reel sometimes from the force of a gale that is whipping scarves and sending dry leaves skittering. But it is all vigorous and gay. And you think—what a glorious thing is skating. Except for skiing, surely the nearest we ever come to flying, personally flying. When we put on skates we are fastening wings to our heels; we become winged gods for a little while, like Mercury. Limited, earthbound, we will never soar by our own power far into the sky like the geese; unlike the ducks we can't even lift and flap off a little way. But we are flying, surely flying on one level, and our spirits soar free.

Maybe your son is right. Maybe it's high time you bought a new pair of skates.

Waltz of the Wind

The snow coasts softly down, steadily, gently, its white ribbons winding the world.

And the wind comes rejoicing to claim it. The wind clasps it in loving arms like a bridegroom his veiled bride for dancing. Together they spin and dip in the wind's waltzing, while now and then the sun, like a happy father, beams upon them.

Night and Fog and Wintry Sea

A winter's evening at the sea. . . .

You struggle along the deserted boardwalk, where only a few lights burn. The wind tries to hurl you ahead, then press you back, as if venting its frustration that it seems unable to strike aside the fog whose wet gray veils have swaddled both sky and sea. The sky is somewhere up there—now and then through a hole you spy a surprised star peering down. The sea is somewhere out there—you can hear it roaring, and know it's there by the foghorn's bleat. But the wind whips around a corner screeching like a gull; for an instant it seems about to lift you, hurl you bodily—thrillingly—into the damp mysterious gray.

To the left shopwindows insist on reality. Most are boarded up for the season, others still parade their wares. SALE, DISCOUNTS, BARGAINS cry the signs, as if to snatch your attention from the enormity, the vast shifting gray enormity that might spirit you away.

Below, through a break in the boardwalk, there is evidence at last of the waves. They come swooping in like an invading horde; white-bearded, white-toothed, they snarl at the sand, then retreat to advance and attack again.

The lighthouse strains against the fog. In the distance its lone eye burns like a misty flower. No, it is more like a woman grieving, for it flings out a fragile arm draped in yellow chiffon, searching, searching. . . . The voice of the foghorn tries to reassure her with its rhythmic deep-toned blattings. There is something both comical and majestic about them. Eerie yet amusing. They make you think of bullfrogs squatting on lily pads, patiently summoning mates. Or a belching Neptune somewhere out there on a watery throne.

You come dripping into a little restaurant of checkered tablecloths and candles and sailors' knots and mighty fish pinioned against rough walls. Enormous sailfish and marlin, glassy-eyed, blue-varnished. A coal fire burns on a blackened grate and the fragrance of coffee and seafood is strong. You shrug out of your coat and pick up the steaming mug they set before you.

Beyond the mullioned windows you hear the sea still dimly grumbling, and the muffled, half-ominous half-merry belling of the horns. How good it is to be here, so close to night and fog and wintry sea, and yet so safe, so snug.

Frosty Morning

There are forests on our windows. Ferns and trees and jungle growths and sweeping vines. A fairyland forest painted there in the night with cold bright brushes dipped in some magic sparkling stuff that only one artist owns.

"Jack Frost!" the children cry. "Look, look—" Breathless, they rush to admire his handiwork, press their cheeks to the glass in a caress as old as time. They pull back at its furry tingling, giggle and boast, "Ouch, that feels good!" You hear their micelike scratching as they scrape holes to peer out on a world that is likewise magic-sketched.

The backyard is like an etching, twigs and bushes and grasses all silver-penciled against the black-brown tones of the ground. The chains of the swings, a ladder propped against the garage, a trashpail with its jauntily crooked lid—these too he has chalked and stenciled and stippled into his lively glittering landscape.

And when you go out across the crisp grass to feed the birds, you find their station jeweled. He has dumped diamonds into his buckets, strewn them lavishly about. The clothesline is a necklace, and all the weeds wear gems.

"Oh, please can Judy stay for dinner tonight?" they beg. "We'll cook it, we'll do everything ourselves."

Bone-weary after a hard day, you're too exhausted to resist. "Okay, fine, Daddy won't be home, get what you want and surprise me."

You hear them clattering around in the kitchen, and except for such minor pleas as, "How long do you cook spaghetti?" and "Are canned beets supposed to be fried or boiled?" they leave you at peace with the paper. And when you finally bestir yourself to face the tray they come proudly toting, you're so tired that even the salty spaghetti and hamburger between two slices of bread and cold beets adorned with parsley actually taste good.

But there's still the neighbor child to be seen home through the darkness and the storm. And when they've finished the dishes you summon the strength to shoo them into wraps, and drag on your own. "Since we're going anyway," you sigh, "we may as well take the dog."

So the Dalmation bounds along, so delighted to be out she drags you skidding at the end of her leash. "Look," the children laugh—and mimic her—"she thinks it's good to eat, she's trying to catch snowflakes with her tongue!"

164

The snow is still twining down. The street lamps shine like fairy torches. Cars creep along, their headlights twin lanes of brightness in the softly whispering world. The icy branches tinkle, turned to wands of glass.

At the neighbor's doorway voices ring out, and laughter—and heading home you are conscious of a strange but sure metamorphosis: Limbs almost too tired to start have become magically light—you lope after the dog and wade the drifts with a sense of sheer fun. A head that ached, a spirit weary, were left somewhere behind in the house.

It is as if the air, so clean and sparkling, the snow like a great white comforter, the vigor of children and the comedy of a prancing dog, have cleansed and rested and refreshed you.

To your own surprise you hear yourself calling, "Let's have a snow-fight. Let's take the sled and coast down the drive. Let's not go in!"

Evergreens

How grateful we should be for evergreens. For the spruces, the firs, the cedars, the pines. All the varieties of trees that refuse to give way to winter, and however bleak the day rest our eyes and restore our spirits with their banners of green.

The sky may be steely gray; yet against it toss the green plumes of the pines. Tall and straight they stand, these "first families" of the trees, an ancient race we are told, dating back to the beginnings of man.

Cone-clotted, the spruces sweep the ground. The blue spruce most nearly reflect the cool colors of winter, for their crisp pointy needles range from blue-green to silvery white. Yet they too lend their lovely green. The firs hold their ripe cones proudly erect, like offerings from their ferny hands. The balsam firs lend their fragrance as well; their sap congeals in perfumed beads; their needles fill pillows that are sweet for sleeping.

Whatever their nature or species, the evergreens help us to hold fast to the hue so vital to our eyes. For green is the color of summer and life when the world is awake and stirring; the color of leaves and vines and grass when the skies are blue and the sun shines warm. "See, see," the evergreens proclaim, "life is not over, only resting, all is not frozen and stripped. Summer will come again and all the greens return. Meanwhile, take comfort in us, look at us and remember some things are eternal." Yes, green is the color of promise and faith.

Green is also the color of Christmas. For it is the prickly living boughs of the evergreens that we carry inside to celebrate. They make our mantels festive, their wreaths adorn our doors. And though some people may find it necessary to substitute artificial trees, no substitute of plastic or silver can duplicate the wonder of a Christmas tree of genuine vibrant green. A tree cut and brought fresh from the forest to stand as a symbol of life—all life. The tender new life of the Christ child—or any child, in the cradle. We can almost hear the tree breathing, speaking to us in little friendly whisperings in the night. And when we come in from the cold and sniff its sweet tang, we feel refreshed and joyous.

How grateful we can be. When the rest of the world is resting, stripped and bare and bleak, how lucky we are to have these faithful beauties. How good of God to give us evergreens.

The Queen Wore Icicles Too

Two warriors are jousting in the yard. They are clad in the latest garb for duelers—blue jeans, plaid jackets. One wears a helmet of leather with flopping ear flaps, the other is bareheaded (he must have lost his cap, you'll scold him later). But their mittened hands grasp mighty weapons that glisten in the sun: Icicles wrenched from the vast dripping arsenal under the bridge.

They prance about, brandishing their glassy swords. They stab and lunge and thrust. There is a clash, a merry shattering; the glittering fragments of their weapons fly. Except for the stumps they are useless now, though one boy (yours) begins to lick the one he holds.

Before you can run to the door to stop him he's thrown it down. Not too dirty (he wouldn't mind that a bit), too cold. He attempts to warm his tongue on a sleeve. Then the two of them go scrambling and skidding down the steep creek bank, to slide on the thin sheet there, to stamp its crackling edges before dipping (now more like swallows) under the bridge. You can visualize their awed prowling, hear their echoing shouts. For there, as in the remembered caves and culverts of your own childhood, the icicles hang like enchanted forests upside down. . . .

The Ice King's own domain. . . . A place where you could feel his hoary breath and sense his shivering power. Where you could dimly hear the clang of his chariot wheels approaching across frozen wastes, and the whistling whips of wind that lashed on his snowy steeds. . . . And his eyes were steely blue, his beard frost-white and fringed with icicles that made a fearful chiming as he dashed past.

His Queen wore icicles too. Sometimes as ornaments for her hair, always as fringe for her white velvet dresses and ermine wraps. She often hung her wardrobe under the eaves of the back porch for you to admire. And the King sometimes hurled his weapons there too—thick glassy clubs, lancets and spears. How amazing to find they had chosen your own back porch for this purpose; it was a secret they asked you never to tell, and you never did, for they were your friends. Though the Queen was much nicer to know than the King, whom you always feared.

You feel suddenly close to them again. They have come back with the jousting of small warriors in the yard.

Sunday Afternoon

It's fun to be a woman when friends drop in on a Sunday afternoon, when for once, you've tidied up the house after church.

Crackling and quarreling like children playing leapfrog, a fire is going. You have even just made a big fresh pot of coffee, and there are plenty of cookies and fruitcake on hand.

As you sit chatting and drinking coffee, the gray clouds outside part as if to make way—and the sun appears, like some shining potentate. Its brilliance fills the room.

It plays across the polished floor, the breath of the rug. It explores the piano, touches the plants and cups and caresses the faces of your friends. It is like some remarkable presence that has peered in, seen the sociable fire, the people, and decided to join.

Yet even as the sun is making himself at home, snowflakes begin to coast across the banners he has trailed outdoors. They dart this way and that, glittering like aimless little lost figures cast out of their cloudy homes. Their tiny lanterns twinkle, hunting their way.

"Look, look, it's snowing!" people remark. "How lovely." And it is. As if all this has been arranged by some decorator or master stagehand as a backdrop for the enhancement of your beautiful afternoon.

Snow Shadows

You awake to a white-furred world. The shrubs and bushes beside the house are bowed with the lovely burden. Wrapped in ermine, decked in diamonds, they twinkle in the sun. While the gaudy little berries of the Pyracantha pop through like rubies, glittering.

Across all this loveliness lie the shadows, in stripes and lacey traceries. And across these leaning shadows dart the quick silhouettes of the birds. They land on a laden branch, sparrows and starlings and cardinals and jays. Then off they flit to the sun-striped fence or the feeding station to peck and quarrel over the bread crusts, the suet and the seeds.

Hearing the shrill chatter and laughter of children, you expect to see them sledding. Instead, there are three of them arching gaily back and forth in their snow-muffled swings.

Showers of white fall from the bars overhead, and they kick up small snowstorms with their feet. A plaid scarf blows, the tassel on a scarlet stocking cap bounces, mittened hands grasp the silvery chains. What rare delight, what unusual fun!

Like three frantic little pendulums moving at different speeds they hurtle back and forth, laughing and shrieking at the showers that cascade down upon them, and the snowy explosions below that their kicking boots create.

Winter's Raiment

The snow lies smooth and untrodden, its white expanse unmarred by any print save perhaps the delicate tracery of a rabbit . . . as soft and secret as the snow itself.

The snow glints with a million little points that grow brighter as the sun rises—as if pleased with itself, growing more bold in its self-delight. . . .

All the trees are furred with it, the smallest branch bearing its precious ermine carefully against the wind.

Now and then little veils of it come cascading down, and the trees become graceful dancers, half-hidden, half-revealed through their wheeling draperies.

Storybook Sledding

The streets at the bottom of the hill have been closed off to traffic and the children are sledding. "Come watch us," they beg. "Come too!"

You hear their shouts and laughter and the inevitable arguments as you go tramping across the yard, see their bright cluster of sleds, stocking caps, mittens and scarves. It is a Christmas card come alive, it is an old picture from Dickens or Whittier or the "Saturday Evening Post." It is your own childhood, the ghosts of winters past and winters to come.

Little folks bounce and tease for turns. Older ones arrogantly hurl themselves flat and go skimming and weaving down the shining slopes. Their runners glisten in the last rays of the sun.

"Hey, Mom, you try it," a son invites. "Get on behind me, I'll steer." Gingerly you mount the sled and are off on the perilous journey, hearing the hum and hiss of steel, feeling the tingling kiss of wind on your face. And when you've come trudging back, exhilarated, he insists you take it by yourself. This is even more exciting; now you too are belly-down to the bumps, nose to the whistling tracks, maneuvering, careening, swerving wildly while trees and fences flash past.

You skid at last to a stop near the barricades.

They stand, sturdy dark angles of protection, lantern-hung. There is a kind of simple beauty about their lean stance. You linger against them a moment, catching your breath, gazing up at the flock of storybook figures on the hill, and the next to come winging down.

New Eyes with Which to See

Give me new eyes with which to see the New Year, Lord. Give me new and clearer vision. Let me bring new awareness to all the dear and precious sights and sounds about me, greet them with new delight, new enthusiasm. Let no day pass without my remarking on the beauty and wonder of all that is about me—from a bug (even a bug in my kitchen) to a budding tree, from a chipped saucepan heaped with apples for peeling to a Van Gogh in a gallery.

Lord, don't let me take for granted a single moment of a single day of this coming year. Keep my eyes bright for seeing, my ears alert for listening, so that I live in a state of awareness, always ready to receive the beauty that is there.

Let me observe as a painter, hear as a composer, live as a performer in the greatest drama ever written, enacted on the most marvelous stage. You have made the world so incredibly lovely, designed it so skillfully, adorned it so exquisitely. And you have lavished your artistry not only on mountains in their majesty, seas in their splendor, forests in their grandeur—but on the simplest, humblest things about me: A mud puddle in the sun. A child with a pair of skates. The peeling door of an abandoned house. A single tree.

Thank you for all these wonders, Lord. For those I have witnessed in the past, and those that await me in this exciting New Year.

A Way of Mists with Snow

In how many ways the world beautifies itself for us. How often it offers some different, delightful, all too brief attraction. A unique combination of light or sun or shadow, a way of mists with snow.

Saturday the snow turns to rain and nightfall brings a heavy fog. It is difficult to creep through it coming home at midnight. Snowdrifts by the roadside, fogdrifts all about. Together they have a quality vaguely exciting, vaguely ominous as your headlights thrust through them anxiously or they are speared by other lights approaching. Their soft hands are not consoling. They pat the landscape into oblivion, dissolve and almost eradicate the road.

Then Sunday morning the sun is shining gaily. And setting off for church you find last night's enemies combining forces to present sheer loveliness. For above the snowy fields and yards hovers an innocent twinkling mist. It is all gossamer and delicate and as happy as the sunshine now. And the snowy expanse that lies beneath it wears it with an air of sweet allurement. While all else is sparkling and newly defined—road, houses, churches, trees— each vivid among the flirting veils, newly radiant and clear as if to compensate.

Thank Goodness for Guests

A housewife's hope never seems highest or brightest than when she's just cleaned up the house for oncoming guests.

She stands for one long sweet moment surveying this little miracle of loveliness: Not a crumb on the rug, not a paper out of place.

No clutter of toys, magazines, pencils, ironing, sewing or homework offends her happy gaze. (All have been hidden in closets, stuffed into drawers, thrust under beds.)

No strewn garments (the offspring have been bullied into hanging them up or getting them into clothes hampers for a change.) No Scout projects, apple cores, rollers, or library books.

The furniture has been polished until it winks; the very floors beam back at her. Through open doors she can see her prettiest towels adorning the bathroom.

Even the clutter of cooking for company has been beaten into submission; the kitchen itself is sheer sweet magazine-picture charm and order. While from piano, mantel and coffee table, flowers add their gay splashes of color.

"Why, it is beautiful!" she marvels. "Why don't we KEEP it this way?" And for one mad and giddy moment, it occurs to her: You COULD. If everybody would just begin picking up after himself.

If you, yourself, would take a final sweep about the premises before bedtime, tidying up. If you'd remember to scrub the stove every time you use it, and pop dirty dishes into the dishwasher at once. . . .

And why not flowers every day—or at least a bright plant strategically placed? And a fire like that crackling on the hearth? And . . . and . . .

But even as her bright plans leap, a silly little being begins to wring its helpless hands. "Towels like that were never meant for hands just out of finger paint," it seems to say. "Who'd haul in the wood and clean the fireplace? You know that fruit-in-a-bowl arrangement in the kitchen wouldn't last five minutes when the kids got home from school. . . ."

She refuses to listen to it. Right now, in all this rare and lovely order, she is a magazine-picture wife, mother, hostess. And if for that reason, and that reason only—well, thank goodness for guests!

Christmas Stars

On the way home from church the littlest one presses her nose against the glass. "Jesus had to be born at Christmas," she announces. "Because there's more stars then."

"Not more stars," corrects a brother, as they pile out of the car. "There's always the same number of stars, isn't there, Mother? And they didn't even *name* it Christmas till after he was born."

"All right, winter." She slides happily along the jeweled walk. "There had to be lots more stars so the shepherds could see them."

"I just *told* you—there couldn't be any more stars. Maybe it just seems like it because in winter the stars seem brighter."

"Why? Do stars like cold weather? Is that why they light up their fires more and sparkle better?"

"I give up." With a playful spank he turns her over to you and plunges on into the house.

You take her mittened hand and stand for a moment sharing her fascination with the sky. It is like a vast meadow tonight, strewn with a million star daisies. And roses carved from sapphires. And silver cockleburs. A few get tangled and lost in shifting white thickets of clouds, and a few have dipped so close they seem caught in the fingers of the trees. They flash enticingly there, almost close enough to pluck.

"*Do* stars really sparkle more at Christmas, Mother?" she persists.

"Yes," you tell her, "I think they do."

"I bet I know why."

"Okay, why?"

"Because it's a time when everybody *feels* sparkly when they look!"

ABOUT THE AUTHOR

MARJORIE HOLMES is the author of many successful books, among them *I've Got to Talk to Somebody, God; Who Am I, God?; How Can I Find You, God; Two From Galilee* and, most recently, *Hold Me Up a Little Longer, Lord*. Miss Holmes has taught writing courses at Catholic University in Maryland, the Georgetown Summer Writers Conference and the Cape Cod Summer Writers Conference, among others. A native of Iowa, she is a graduate of Cornell College in that state. She has traveled widely, recently visiting Israel in connection with the forthcoming motion picture of *Two From Galilee*. Miss Holmes (Mrs. Lynn Mighell in private life) is the mother of four grown children. She and her husband make their home on Lake Jackson in Manassas, Virginia.

Heartwarming Books
of
Faith and Inspiration

☐	12674	**POSITIVE PRAYERS FOR POWER-FILLED LIVING** Robert H. Schuller	$1.95
☐	13269	**THE GOSPEL ACCORDING TO PEANUTS** Robert L. Short	$1.75
☐	13266	**HOW CAN I FIND YOU, GOD?** Marjorie Holmes	$1.95
☐	10947	**THE FINDING OF JASPER HOLT** Grace Livingston Hill	$1.50
☐	12483	**THE BIBLE AS HISTORY** Werner Keller	$2.95
☐	12218	**THE GREATEST MIRACLE IN THE WORLD** Og Mandino	$1.95
☐	12009	**THE GREATEST SALESMAN IN THE WORLD** Og Mandino	$1.95
☐	12330	**I'VE GOT TO TALK TO SOMEBODY, GOD** Marjorie Holmes	$1.95
☐	12853	**THE GIFT OF INNER HEALING** Ruth Carter Stapleton	$1.95
☐	12444	**BORN AGAIN** Charles Colson	$2.50
☐	13436	**SHROUD** Robert Wilcox	$2.50
☐	13366	**A GRIEF OBSERVED** C. S. Lewis	$2.25
☐	13077	**TWO FROM GALILEE** Marjorie Holmes	$2.25
☐	12717	**LIGHTHOUSE** Eugenia Price	$1.95
☐	12835	**NEW MOON RISING** Eugenia Price	$1.95
☐	13003	**THE LATE GREAT PLANET EARTH** Hal Lindsey	$2.25

Buy them at your local bookstore or use this handy coupon for ordering: